The Battle of Gettysburg

Books in the Battles Series:

The Battle of Belleau Wood
The Battle of Britain
The Battle of Gettysburg
The Battle of Hastings
The Battle of Marathon

The Battle of Midway
The Battle of Waterloo
The Battle of Zama
The Inchon Invasion
The Invasion of Normandy

✫ Battles of the Civil War ✫

The Battle of Gettysburg

by James A. Corrick

C. 1

Lucent Books, P.O. Box 289011, San Diego, CA 92198-9011

For Maggie,

Whose comments made this a better book

Library of Congress Cataloging-in-Publication Data

Corrick, James A.
    The Battle of Gettysburg / by James A. Corrick.
      p. cm. — (Battles of the Civil War)
    Includes bibliographical references and index.
    Summary: Provides a detailed account of this decisive battle of
the Civil War including events leading up to it, the course of the
battle itself, and its consequences.
    ISBN 1-56006-451-X (alk. paper)
      1. Gettysburg (Pa.), Battle of, 1863—Juvenile literature.
    [1. Gettysburg (Pa.), Battle of, 1863. 2. United States—History—
Civil War, 1861–1865—Campaigns.] I. Title. II. Series.
    E475.53.C79 1996
    973.7'349—dc20
                                                    95-31681
                                                       CIP
                                                        AC

Contents

Foreword

Almost everyone would agree with William Tecumseh Sherman that war "is all hell." Yet the history of war, and battles in particular, is so fraught with the full spectrum of human emotion and action that it becomes a microcosm of the human experience. Soldiers' lives are condensed and crystallized in a single battle. As Francis Miller explains in his *Photographic History of the Civil War* when describing the war wounded, "It is sudden, the transition from marching bravely at morning on two sound legs, grasping your rifle in two sturdy arms, to lying at nightfall under a tree with a member forever gone."

Decisions made on the battlefield can mean the lives of thousands. A general's pique or indigestion can result in the difference between life and death. Some historians speculate, for example, that Napoleon's fateful defeat at Waterloo was due to the beginnings of stomach cancer. His stomach pain may have been the reason that the normally decisive general was sluggish and reluctant to move his troops. And what kept George McClellan from winning battles during the Civil War? Some scholars and contemporaries believe that it was simple cowardice and fear. Others argue that he felt a gut-wrenching unwillingness to engage in the war of attrition that was characteristic of that particular conflict.

Battle decisions can be magnificently brilliant and horribly costly. At the Battle of Thaspus in 47 B.C., for example, Julius Caesar, facing a numerically superior army, shrewdly ordered his troops onto a narrow strip of land bordering the sea. Just as he expected, his enemy thought he had accidentally trapped himself and divided their forces to surround his troops. By dividing their army, his enemy had given Caesar the strategic edge he needed to defeat them. Other battle orders result in disaster, as in the case of the Battle at Balaklava during the Crimean War in 1854. A British general gave the order to attack a force of withdrawing enemy Russians. But confusion in relaying the order resulted in the 670 men of the Light Brigade's charging in the wrong direction into certain death by heavy enemy cannon fire. Battles are the stuff of history on the grandest scale—their outcomes often determine whether nations are enslaved or liberated.

Moments in battles illustrate the best and worst of human character. In the feeling of terror and the us-versus-them attitude that accompanies war, the enemy can be dehumanized and treated with a contempt that is considered repellent in times of peace. At Wounded Knee, the distrust and anticipation of violence that grew between the Native Americans and American soldiers led to the senseless killing of ninety men, women, and children. And who can forget My Lai, where the deaths of old men, women, and children at the hands of American soldiers shocked an America already disillusioned with the Vietnam War. The murder of six million Jews will remain burned into the human conscience forever as the measure of man's inhumanity to man. These horrors cannot be forgotten. And yet, under the terrible conditions of battle, one can find acts of bravery, kindness, and altruism. During the Battle of Midway, the members of Torpedo Squadron 8, flying in hopelessly antiquated planes and without the benefit of air protection from fighters, tried bravely to fulfill their mission—to destroy the *Kido Butai,* the Japanese Carrier Striking Force. Without air support, the squadron was immediately set upon by Japanese fighters. Nevertheless, each bomber tried valiantly to hit his target. Each failed. Every man but one died in the effort. But by keeping the Japanese fighters busy, the squadron bought time and delayed further Japanese fighter attacks. In the aftermath of the Battle of Isandhlwana in South Africa in 1879, a force of thousands of Zulu warriors trapped a contingent of British troops in a small trading post. After repeated bloody attacks in which many died on both sides, the Zulus, their final victory certain, granted the remaining British their lives as a gesture of respect for their bravery. During World War I, American troops were so touched by the fate of French war orphans that they took up a collection to help them. During the Civil War, soldiers of the North and South would briefly forget that they were enemies and share smokes and coffee across battle lines during the endless nights. These acts seem all the more dramatic, more uplifting, because they indicate that people can continue to behave with humanity when faced with inhumanity.

Lucent Books' Battles Series highlights the vast range of the human character revealed in the ordeal of war. Dramatic narrative describes in exciting and accurate detail the commanders, soldiers, weapons, strategies, and maneuvers involved in each battle. Each volume includes a comprehensive historical context, explaining what brought the parties to war, the events leading to the battle, what factors made the battle important, and the effects it had on the larger war and later events.

The Battles Series also includes a chronology of important dates that gives students an overview, at a glance, of each battle. Sidebars create a broader context by adding enlightening details on leaders, institutions, customs, warships, weapons, and armor mentioned in the narration. Every volume contains numerous maps that allow readers to better visualize troop movements and strategies. In addition, numerous primary and secondary source quotations drawn from both past historical witnesses and modern historians are included. These quotations demonstrate to readers how and where historians derive information about past events. Finally, the volumes in the Battles Series provide a launching point for further reading and research. Each book contains a bibliography designed for student research, as well as a second bibliography that includes the works the author consulted while compiling the book.

Above all, the Battles Series helps illustrate the words of Herodotus, the fifth-century B.C. Greek historian now known as the "father of history." In the opening lines of his great chronicle of the Greek and Persian Wars, the world's first battle book, he set for himself this goal: "To preserve the memory of the past by putting on record the astonishing achievements both of our own and of other peoples; and more particularly, to show how they came into conflict."

Chronology of Events

1861

April 12   War breaks out when Confederate forces fire on Fort Sumter in the harbor of Charleston, South Carolina.

April 19   Abraham Lincoln orders a naval blockade of the Confederacy.

July 21   Confederate forces defeat Union troops at the First Battle of Bull Run near Manassas, Virginia.

November 1   Union general George B. McClellan creates the Army of the Potomac.

1862

February 25   Union troops capture Nashville, Tennessee.

April 4   The Army of the Potomac begins the Peninsular campaign, an attempt to capture Richmond, Virginia.

April 6–7   Union forces commanded by Ulysses S. Grant win the Battle of Shiloh in Tennessee.

April 25   Union naval forces under the command of David Farragut capture New Orleans.

June 1   Confederate president Jefferson Davis appoints Robert E. Lee commander of Confederate forces at Richmond; Lee names his new command the Army of Northern Virginia.

June 6   Union forces capture Memphis, Tennessee.

June 25–July 1   The Peninsular campaign ends when the Army of Northern Virginia drives the Army of the Potomac away from Richmond in the Seven Days' Battles.

August 29–30   The Army of Northern Virginia defeats the Army of the Potomac at the Second Battle of Bull Run.

September 17   The Army of the Potomac defeats the Army of Northern Virginia at the Battle of Antietam near Sharpsburg, Maryland.

September 22   Lincoln issues the Emancipation Proclamation, which frees all slaves in the Confederate states.

December 13   The Army of Northern Virginia defeats the Army of the Potomac at the Battle of Fredericksburg in Virginia.

1863

May 1–4   The Army of Northern Virginia defeats the Army of the Potomac at the Battle of Chancellorsville in Virginia; Confederate general Thomas "Stonewall" Jackson is mortally wounded.

May 18   Union forces under Grant besiege Vicksburg.

June 3   The Gettysburg campaign gets under way when the Army of Northern Virginia marches north.

June 9   Confederate cavalry units commanded by General Jeb Stuart drive off Union cavalry at Brandy Station, Virginia.

June 13   The Army of the Potomac follows Lee's army north.

June 14   The Army of Northern Virginia's Second Corps, commanded by General Richard S. Ewell, drives off the Union garrison at Winchester, Virginia.

June 15   The Army of Northern Virginia crosses the Potomac River into Maryland.

June 24   Advance units of the Army of Northern Virginia reach Pennsylvania; Lee loses contact with Stuart and his cavalry units.

June 26   Lee establishes his headquarters at Chambersburg, Pennsylvania.

June 28   General George Meade becomes commander of the Army of the Potomac.

June 29   Meade and the Army of the Potomac arrive at Pipe Creek, near Taneytown, Maryland.

June 30

Noon   Union cavalry under the command of General John Buford reaches Gettysburg.

7:30 p.m.   Buford's force drives off Confederate units from the Army of Northern Virginia's Third Corps.

July 1

5:30 a.m.   Confederate general Henry Heth of Third Corps attacks Buford's cavalry, beginning the Battle of Gettysburg.

9:00 a.m.   The Union soldiers take up a position on McPherson's Ridge.

10:00 a.m.   General John Reynolds and part of the Army of the Potomac's First Corps arrive at Gettysburg.

10:30 a.m.   Reynolds is killed by a Confederate sharpshooter, and General Abner Doubleday assumes command.

11:30 a.m.   Union troops throw back Heth's attack on McPherson's Ridge, capturing Confederate general James Archer.

Noon The Army of the Potomac's Eleventh Corps arrives at Gettysburg, with General Oliver Howard taking command from Doubleday; the Confederates begin heavy shelling of Union lines.

2:00 p.m.   General Robert Rodes of the Army of Northern Virginia's Second Corps attacks the Union position, but the Union line holds.

2:15 p.m.   Meade sends General Winfield Scott Hancock to look over the battleground at Gettysburg.

2:30 p.m.   Lee arrives at Gettysburg and surveys the ongoing battle, unsure of whether he wants to continue the fight.

3:30 p.m.   General Jubal Early joins Rodes's attack against the Union troops, breaking the Federal line and forcing the northern soldiers to retreat; Lee decides to stay and fight at Gettysburg.

4:00 p.m.   Retreating Union forces dig in on top of Cemetery Hill.

4:15 p.m. Hancock arrives at Gettysburg and orders the occupation of nearby Culp's Hill.

4:30 p.m. Lee requests that Ewell attack Cemetery Hill, but Ewell does not attack.

5:30 p.m. Hancock sends Meade a message advising the northern commander to commit the entire Army of the Potomac to the battle.

July 2

3:00 a.m. Meade arrives at Gettysburg.

4:00 a.m. Meade positions Union troops along Cemetery Ridge.

8:00 a.m. The first two divisions of the Army of Northern Virginia's First Corps arrive at Gettysburg.

9:00 a.m. Lee receives report that Meade had not occupied Little Round Top.

Noon Generals John B. Hood and Lafayette McLaws of the First Corps begin positioning their troops for an attack on Cemetery Ridge.

3:00 p.m. Union general Daniel Sickles moves Third Corps off Cemetery Ridge and into the Peach Orchard.

4:00 p.m. Hood attacks Sickles's Third Corps in Peach Orchard, and fighting spreads to Devil's Den.

5:00 p.m. Union defenders reach Little Round Top.

5:15 p.m. The Confederates attack Little Round Top.

5:30 p.m. McLaws joins the attack against Third Corps.

6:00 p.m. Sickles is seriously wounded and leaves the field; Richard H. Anderson of Third Corps attacks Union center on Cemetery Ridge.

6:15 p.m. Union troops secure Little Round Top.

7:30 p.m. The Confederate attack fails to break the Federal line on Cemetery Ridge, and the Confederates retreat.

8:00 p.m. Generals Jubal Early and Edward Johnson of Second Corps attack Union positions on Cemetery and Culp's Hills.

10:30 p.m. Early's soldiers retreat from Cemetery Hill.

11:00 p.m. Johnson's troops occupy a part of Culp's Hill; Meade and his staff meet to plan the next day's fighting.

July 3

4:30 a.m. Union artillery bombards Johnson's troops on Culp's Hill.

5:30 a.m. Johnson's troops launch counterattack against Federal soldiers on Culp's Hill.

Noon The last Confederates retreat from Culp's Hill.

1:00 p.m. Confederate artillery blasts away at the center of the Union line on Cemetery Ridge.

3:00 p.m. Confederate artillery barrages cease, and General George Pickett of First Corps attacks the Federal troops on Cemetery Ridge.

3:20 p.m. Pickett's soldiers come under heavy fire from Federal artillery.

3:45 p.m. Confederate and Union troops fight at the Angle; Hancock is wounded and carried from the field.

4:00 p.m. Pickett's troops retreat from Cemetery Ridge, ending the Battle of Gettysburg.

July 4 The Army of Northern Virginia begins its retreat back to Virginia; in the west, Grant's troops take Vicksburg.

July 14 The Army of Northern Virginia crosses the Potomac back into Confederate territory.

July 27 The Gettysburg campaign ends when the Army of Northern Virginia and the Army of the Potomac set up camps near Culpeper, Virginia.

September 19–20 Confederate forces defeat Union troops at the Battle of Chickamauga in Tennessee.

November 19 Lincoln delivers his Gettysburg Address.

November 23–25 Union forces win the Battle of Chattanooga, Tennessee.

1864

March 9 Lincoln makes Grant general in chief of the U.S. Army.

May 5–7 Grant and the Army of the Potomac engage Lee and the Army of Northern Virginia at the Battle of the Wilderness in Virginia; although Grant loses the battle, he advances toward Richmond.

June 16–18 The Army of the Potomac besieges Petersburg, Virginia, just south of Richmond.

September 2 Union general William T. Sherman's troops capture Atlanta.

December 21 Sherman captures Savannah, Georgia.

1865

March 30–April 1 The Army of the Potomac defeats the Army of Northern Virginia at the Battle of Five Forks in Virginia.

April 2 Union forces take Petersburg and then Richmond; Davis and the Confederate government flee.

April 9 Lee surrenders to Grant at Appomattox Court House, Virginia.

April 14 John Wilkes Booth mortally wounds Lincoln at Ford's Theater; Union troops hold victory celebration at Fort Sumter.

April 26 Confederate general Joseph E. Johnston surrenders to Sherman.

May 10 Union cavalry captures Jefferson Davis in Georgia.

May 13 Confederate forces defeat Union troops at Palmito Ranch, Texas, in the final battle of the war.

May 26 Union general Edward Canby accepts the surrender of the last active Confederate troops.

INTRODUCTION

A Crucial Battle: A Defeat Here Would Be Ruinous

The Battle of Gettysburg, July 1–3, 1863, was combat on an epic scale. Fought during the American Civil War (1861–1865) near the small farm town of Gettysburg, Pennsylvania, this battle was the largest and bloodiest ever waged in North America.

Historian Bruce Catton observes that the Battle of Gettysburg has come "to symbolize all the war. It was, as if the blunders and heroism, the hopes and delusions [of the Civil War] . . . had been summed up . . . in one monstrous act of violence."

Large and bloody though it was, the Battle of Gettysburg did not end the Civil War. It was fought at the midpoint of the war, and two more years of hard fighting and terrible battles remained before the United States defeated the Confederate States of America.

Gettysburg played an important role in that final victory and that final defeat. Losing the Battle of Gettysburg prevented the Confederate States from ending the war in 1863. Winning at Gettysburg gave the United States the will to continue fighting until its eventual victory in 1865.

North and South

The road to Gettysburg began two years before when eleven Southern states seceded from the United States to form their own country, the Confederate States of America, also known as the Confederacy. These states were Alabama, Arkansas, Florida, Georgia, Louisiana, Mississippi, North Carolina, South Carolina,

Tennessee, Texas, and Virginia. Each believed that its very way of life would be destroyed if it remained part of the United States.

Many issues led to secession, but they all had their roots in the different ways of life found in the South and the North. The South was almost entirely a farming region and supported few factories. Its main crops were cotton and tobacco, which were sold to the Northern states and all over the world. The farming economy of the South depended on the labor of 3.5 million black slaves. These slaves made up over one-third of the total nine million people living in the South.

The Civil War, including the Battle of Gettysburg, was fought because of the increasing differences between the South and the North. As the North became industrialized and had no need for slaves, the South continued to rely on slave labor (lower) to maintain and harvest its crops.

The North, particularly along the Atlantic Ocean, depended on its factories to support the region's population of twenty-three million. Much of the money earned from Southern crops went to buy farm equipment, clothing, and other goods from Northern factories.

In the years before 1860, the social and economic differences between South and North gave rise to much political conflict. The Northern states did not condone slavery, and slavery became the symbol of this conflict.

Although prejudice against blacks existed nationwide, vocal activists in the North, known as abolitionists, called for the abolishment of slavery. Southerners believed that the elimination of slavery would destroy their society and their economy. They also resented outsiders who dictated how they should live.

In November 1860 Abraham Lincoln was elected president. Lincoln belonged to the abolitionist Republican Party, and the South saw his election as the first step toward the destruction of Southern society. Within six weeks of the election, South Carolina became the first Southern state to secede from the United States.

The North Takes Up Arms

As president of the United States, or the Union, Lincoln refused to recognize the Confederacy as a separate country. The U.S. federal government was prepared to declare war in order to force the

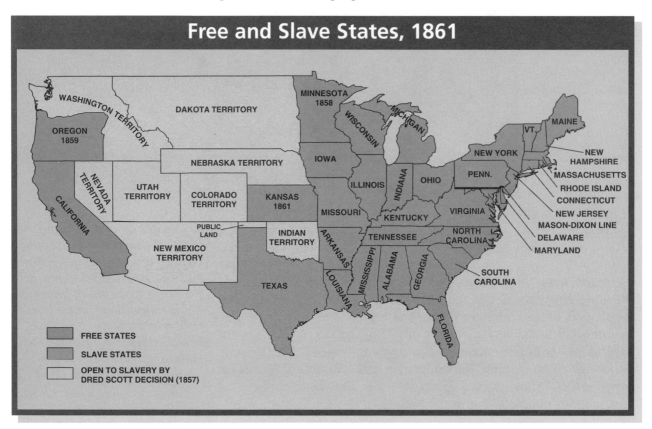

Free and Slave States, 1861

FREE STATES

SLAVE STATES

OPEN TO SLAVERY BY DRED SCOTT DECISION (1857)

Southern states to rejoin the Union. The Confederate States were just as determined to fight for their independence. War began on April 12, 1861, when Confederate forces fired on the Union's Fort Sumter in the harbor of Charleston, South Carolina.

The Union's military strategy had three goals. In the east, the Federal army set out to capture Richmond, Virginia, the capital of the Confederacy. In the west, it determined to take control of the Mississippi River, thus splitting the Confederacy in two. At sea, the Federal navy blockaded the Confederacy. The Union navy's ships cruised along the Confederate coast and kept ships from reaching Southern ports with supplies of guns and other scarce goods.

The South Defends Itself

The Confederacy, on the other hand, fought a more defensive war. The South's goal was to wear down the North until the latter abandoned its desire to force the Southern states back into the Union.

President Abraham Lincoln led the Union in the Civil War. Lincoln's election, which signaled a move toward abolition, sparked the South's decision to secede.

George Washington had successfully used a defensive strategy during the Revolutionary War. He rarely attacked unless he held an overwhelming advantage. Washington constantly retreated, even if it meant giving up American territory; he feared that large battles would destroy his small colonial army.

Washington and his soldiers picked off small units of British troops so that the English suffered a continuous loss of men and supplies, while the strength of the colonial army remained relatively constant. Eventually the war simply cost the British too much for them to continue to fight.

A defensive strategy made good sense for the Confederacy. First, the smaller Southern population could not muster as large an army as the Union. Second, Confederate soldiers would be defending their homes, a factor that would fuel their determination to win. Third, to take the war into the Union would mean long supply and communication lines that would be difficult to protect from Federal attack.

If the South had adopted a completely defensive strategy along the lines of George Washington's, it might well have won the war. However, the Confederate people would not support a military policy based solely on defense, nor would they accept retreat as a major part of that policy. Such strategy seemed too cowardly. As the *Richmond Examiner* wrote, "The idea of waiting

The First Battle of Bull Run put an end to the North's wild optimism that it could defeat the South soundly and quickly. While picnickers watched the action, the vastly outnumbered Southern troops defeated the North.

for blows, instead of inflicting them, is altogether unsuited to the genius [nature] of our people."

In the end the South adopted a defensive-offensive strategy. Whenever possible, Southern troops marched out and fought major battles against invading Northern soldiers. Further, if the opportunity presented itself, the Confederates willingly attacked Northern troops. Because the Confederacy had practically no navy, it could do little to break the Union's naval blockade.

The War Drags On

In the east the Confederate army consistently beat back Union invasions, beginning on July 21, 1861, with the First Battle of Bull Run near Manassas, Virginia. In the west, Union forces gained ground, particularly in Tennessee and along the Mississippi River. In April 1862 Union soldiers captured New Orleans, the largest Confederate city.

Neither side, however, seemed able to score a final and decisive victory. Frustration at the Union's inability to smash the Confederacy mounted in the North as the war dragged on into its third year. Many in the Union were growing tired of the conflict, and the Confederacy's strategy of wearing down the North seemed to be working.

Dark Times for the Union

At the beginning of 1863, Union morale was at an all-time low. Even the most patriotic Northerners had come to doubt that the North could win the war. On January 14, for instance, the *Chicago Tribune*, an enthusiastic supporter of the war, printed that "an armistice [truce] is bound to come during the year '63. The rebs [the Confederates] can't be conquered by the present machinery [army]."

This same gloom also ran through the Northern army. "The army is tired with its hard and terrible experience," wrote Captain Oliver Wendell Holmes Jr. "I've pretty much made up my mind that the South has achieved their independence."

Both the *Tribune* and Holmes were bitterly disappointed by the Union's inability to win battles in Virginia and to capture Richmond. Over the previous two years, the people of the North had watched one large Federal army after another march into Virginia and come reeling back after being battered by smaller Confederate forces.

The most recent of these military disasters in Virginia, the Battle of Fredericksburg, occurred in December of 1862. General Robert E. Lee's Army of Northern Virginia had soundly beaten General Ambrose E. Burnside's Army of the Potomac. Lee only had 78,000 soldiers to Burnside's 115,000, and yet Union losses were 13,000, almost three times greater than Confederate casualties. Even the more successful Union campaign along the Mississippi River ground to a halt in late 1862.

Robert E. Lee continued to deal defeats to the Union army in spite of the Union's superior forces. Lee had an advantage in morale, however—early in the war, the South fought a defensive war on home soil.

Politics and War in the North

As the third year of fighting began, the series of Union defeats in Virginia plunged President Abraham Lincoln into deep political trouble. The president's influence over both the U.S. Congress and the Northern states was now very weak. One contemporary political observer noted that "if a Republican convention were to be held tomorrow, he [Lincoln] would not get the vote of a single state."

Additionally, defeats such as Fredericksburg gave birth to a growing peace movement that demanded an instant end to the war even if peace meant recognizing the Confederacy as a separate nation. Many in the North were revolted by the bloodbaths that Civil War battles had turned out to be. To them, the whole idea of

Union, reuniting North and South, was an abstraction not worth the cost in lives.

Peace candidates were running for governorships and state legislative seats in the fall of 1863, and many seemed certain of winning. States run by antiwar leaders might refuse to send men and supplies to fight the war. Antiwar victories in state elections might also help peace candidates win congressional elections and even the presidency in 1864.

Another Union Defeat

Through the spring of 1863, the war continued to go badly for the Union, at least in the east. In May, the Army of the Potomac, now under its new commander, General Joseph "Fighting Joe" Hooker, lost seventeen thousand men in the Battle of Chancellorsville in Virginia. Again the victors were the Army of Northern Virginia and Robert E. Lee. "My God, my God," a horrified Lincoln said, upon receiving the news about Chancellorsville, "what will the country say?"

Not all Union war news was bad. In the west, an army under Ulysses S. Grant had beaten its Confederate foe, and in the spring of 1863, Grant and his army besieged Vicksburg, Mississippi, the last Confederate stronghold on the Mississippi River.

However, the news from the west was slow in reaching the eastern Union states. Additionally, few in the east saw the western war as very important, particularly in light of the continued failure of Federal armies in Virginia. What the Union desperately needed to keep its people committed to the war was a victory in the east, particularly against the seemingly unbeatable Robert E. Lee.

In July the Army of the Potomac had another chance for victory when it once more encountered Robert E. Lee and the Army of Northern Virginia at Gettysburg. It was an encounter that would change the course of the eastern war.

Running Out of Time

In contrast to popular sentiment in the North, general support for the war was strong in the South. Southerners, like Northerners, were disturbed by the bloody cost of battle, but they saw it as necessary to save their homes and families from invasion. Despite two years of hard fighting, their confidence still ran high. During the first half of 1863, few Confederate citizens doubted the South's ability to win the war.

Southern leaders, however, were not as cocky. The South's defensive-offensive strategy was beginning to look like a losing policy. In spite of a series of impressive victories against Union armies in the east, the Confederacy had not been able to destroy the Union's ability to fight. No matter how many men and how much equipment the Northern armies lost, replacement troops were readily available from the large Union population and new supplies were being produced by Northern factories. The Union armies, particularly the Army of the Potomac, remained strong and posed a constant, deadly threat to the Confederacy.

In the South, however, every soldier mattered. The South was taking as many casualties as the Union, but its smaller population could not replenish the troops. At Chancellorsville, the Army of Northern Virginia suffered thirteen thousand casualties.

Casualties were, of course, not confined to enlisted men. The South had started the war with an exceptionally skilled officer corps. Southerners had accounted for a large percentage of the U.S. Army's officers prior to the war, and most of these officers were graduates of the U.S. Military Academy at West Point. By the third year of the war, death and disabling wounds had reduced that corps by an alarming extent. Skilled officers were even harder to replace than ordinary foot soldiers.

Chancellorsville was particularly costly for the Confederacy because there General Thomas "Stonewall" Jackson was accidentally shot by his own men. Jackson, one of the South's most talented military leaders, died several days later due to complications from his wounds. Lee wept when he heard that the man known as "Lee's right arm" was dead.

The Union lost seventeen thousand men in a stunning defeat to the North during the Battle of Chancellorsville. News of such Union defeats led many Northerners to lose patience with the war effort.

Southern Shortages

The South was also running critically short of supplies, from guns to clothes to food. The South's few factories could not keep up with the demands of war, and growing enough food was a problem because Union troops occupied much of the best Southern farmland. Importing supplies and food from other countries was impossible because of the Union naval blockade.

Both the Confederate army and the civilian population suffered from these severe shortages. A clerk in the Confederate War Department in Richmond wrote that "famine is upon us. I have lost twenty pounds, and my wife and children are emaciated [starved]."

Additionally, Confederate money was practically worthless; inflation was running as high as 9,000 percent. Prices soared, and few Southerners could afford goods and food even when they were available.

By the spring of 1863, Lee was having trouble feeding his soldiers. Lee's nephew, Confederate general Fitzhugh Lee, reported that when the commander of the Army of Northern Virginia requested food for his men, the commissary general said, "If General Lee wants rations, let him seek them in Pennsylvania," meaning that Lee should invade the North to get supplies for his army.

And Pennsylvania is exactly where Lee and the Army of Northern Virginia went in the early summer of 1863. Lee had come to the conclusion that the South's waiting game was not going to work and that the only way to win the war was to quickly take the fight to the enemy. Thus, he and his troops marched up through Maryland and into Pennsylvania for their fateful meeting with the Army of the Potomac at Gettysburg.

CHAPTER ONE

The Road to Gettysburg: We Must Conquer a Peace

The fighting was over. Smoke from rifle volleys, artillery barrages, and out-of-control forest fires burning in the surrounding woods mixed and swirled across the ground like a great low-lying fog. Breaks in the smoke showed huddled masses of dead soldiers—some clad in blue uniforms and some in gray. Many of the dead were burned beyond recognition, having been trapped and burned alive in the spreading forest fires.

It was May 6, 1863, and this was the aftermath of the Battle of Chancellorsville in northeastern Virginia. In several days of hard fighting, Robert E. Lee's Confederate Army of Northern Virginia had beaten the Union's Army of the Potomac, a force almost twice the size of the Southern army.

A Costly Victory

Lee and his soldiers had won the battle, but they were no closer to winning the war than they had been in 1861. Despite a series of brilliant victories over the Federal army during the past year, the Confederates had been unable to destroy the Army of the Potomac. Indeed, as Union general Abner Doubleday later wrote about the days following Chancellorsville:

> The close of the Battle of Chancellorsville found the Union army still strong and ready, as soon as reinforcements and supplies arrived. . . .

Robert E. Lee rides among his victorious troops at the Battle of Chancellorsville.

Our army . . . was still [too] formidable in numbers . . . to be effectively assailed [attacked]. . . . The Rebels had obtained a triumph rather than a substantial victory at Chancellorsville. It was gained, too, at ruinous expense of [Confederate] life; and when the battle was over they found themselves too weak to follow up our retreating forces.

The names of the two armies came from the location of their home bases. Thus, the Army of the Potomac operated out of Washington, D.C., on the banks of the Potomac River. The Army of Northern Virginia was stationed at Richmond, Virginia. Other Union armies included the Army of the Ohio and the Army of the Cumberland. The Confederates had the Army of Mississippi and the Army of Tennessee, among others.

To Pierce Deep into Union Territory

If Doubleday was aware of the insufficient numbers of Confederate troops, so was Robert E. Lee. The Southern general had known from the beginning of the war that the Confederacy could not match the Union in men and supplies in a long war. As he wrote to Confederate president Jefferson Davis, "We should not . . . conceal from ourselves that our resources in men are constantly diminishing."

Lee knew that the only way to solve the South's supply and manpower problems was to win the war quickly, and he believed he had a way to do just that. He would lead the Army of Northern Virginia in an invasion of Pennsylvania. Lee later wrote:

I considered the problem in every possible phase [way], and . . . it resolved itself into a choice . . . : either retire to Richmond and stand a siege, which must ultimately have ended in surrender, or to invade Pennsylvania.

However, before Lee could launch such an invasion, he had to get permission from the Confederate government. Ten days after Chancellorsville, the general outlined his plans to Davis and the Southern president's cabinet. He showed them how his proposed invasion of Pennsylvania could end the war and gain the South its independence.

Lee's Earlier Invasion of the Union

If the Confederate government approved the invasion plan, it would be the second invasion of Union territory for Lee and the Army of Northern Virginia. The first invasion in September 1862 had ended in failure.

After beating the Army of the Potomac at the Second Battle of Bull Run near Manassas, Virginia, Lee and the Army of Northern

Dead artillerymen are part of the gruesome aftermath of the battlefields at Antietam. The Union technically won the battle, though the loss of life on both sides was staggering.

Virginia pursued the Federal force into Union territory. The Southern general and his army caught the Army of the Potomac near Sharpsburg, Maryland, where they fought the Battle of Antietam. The battle ended in a technical victory for the Federals but was in reality more of a draw. Lee and his men retreated to Virginia.

The Maryland campaign had failed because of an improbable accident. A Federal trooper found a copy of Lee's battle plans that a Confederate officer had lost. Such an accident was not likely to happen again.

A Risky Business

Lee knew that his proposed invasion of Pennsylvania was risky. Historian Albert A. Nofi notes: "The army would be operating in hostile territory far from its base. A defeat could lead to its complete dissolution [destruction]." Unlike the previous September, the Army of Northern Virginia would not be invading a border state that had many Southern sympathizers and was in many ways like Confederate Virginia. Instead, the Confederate force would be deep in pro-Union territory.

Lee, however, believed that his men could fight their way out of any such situation and that his troops were unbeatable. "There never were such men in an army before," he said of his soldiers. "They will go anywhere and do anything if properly led."

Another danger connected with the invasion of Pennsylvania was the chance that Army of the Potomac commander Joseph Hooker might seize on the absence of the Army of Northern Virginia as an opportunity to march on Richmond, the Confederate

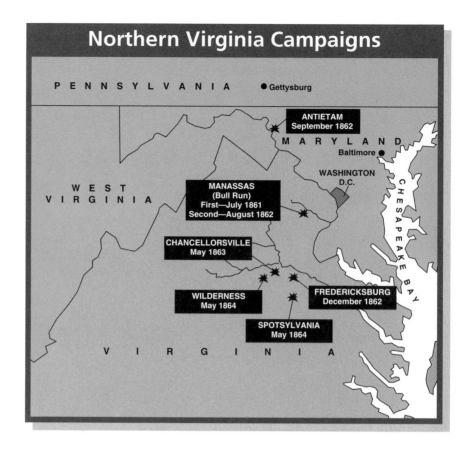

Northern Virginia Campaigns

capital. However, Lee was confident that Hooker would move north in order to keep Union troops between Lee's force and Washington, D.C. According to historian Gene Smith:

> [Lee] did not worry that Hooker would take Richmond, for to do so would entirely uncover Washington. It would be a case of swapping queens, Lee said, and the North could not do that.

To Draw the Enemy Out of Virginia

Lee argued compellingly for his plan. He pointed out to Davis and the cabinet that an invading force in Pennsylvania could threaten not only the Union's capital in Washington, D.C., but also the cities of Baltimore and Philadelphia. The invading force's threat to three major Union cities would draw the Army of the Potomac north from its present camp in Virginia in search of the Army of Northern Virginia.

As a bonus the Union army's withdrawal from Virginia would free local farmers from the constant loss of their crops and livestock to hungry Northern soldiers. Further, the Army of Northern Virginia could resupply itself from the rich farmlands of central Pennsylvania, which were untouched by the war.

Robert E. Lee

Robert Edward Lee, the son of Revolutionary War hero "Light Horse" Harry Lee, was born in Virginia in 1807. Graduating second in his class from West Point in 1829, Lee served in both the U.S. Army engineers and cavalry. He saw action in the 1848 Mexican War, was superintendent of West Point (1852–1855), and led troops that ended John Brown's 1859 raid on Harper's Ferry, Virginia.

In April 1861 Colonel Lee turned down an offer to command all U.S. Army forces. Instead, he resigned and returned to Virginia to become a general in the Confederate army.

In 1861 Lee failed to reconquer the western part of Virginia, which remained loyal to the Union and would become West Virginia. In March 1862 he became Confederate president Jefferson Davis's military advisor, but within a few months, he took command of the Army of Northern Virginia.

After ending a threat from the Army of the Potomac to the Confederate capital of Richmond, Lee beat the Union force in August 1862 at the Second Battle of Bull Run. He invaded Maryland a few weeks later but retreated to Virginia after his army lost the Battle of Antietam.

Prior to the Battle of Gettysburg, he won two more battles against the Army of the Potomac, at Fredericksburg and at Chancellorsville. He continued to command the Army of Northern Virginia after losing at Gettysburg. His soldiers called him Marse Robert, that is, Master Robert.

In the spring of 1864, he began a yearlong series of battles against Union general in chief Ulysses S. Grant. Lee eventually surrendered to Grant at Appomattox Court House in April 1865.

Lee retired to Lexington, Virginia, to become president of Washington College, later to be known as Washington and Lee University. He died in 1870 of the heart disease that had plagued him throughout much of the war.

A brilliant strategist, Lee was able to keep up the South's morale by continually beating his Union opponents.

Lee's prime goal, however, was to lure the Army of the Potomac north, where he would try to force it into battle. If he could win such a battle—and he was completely confident that he and his men could—then he foresaw a number of benefits that could help the South win the war.

Vicksburg Needs Help

The first benefit of invasion was an end to Union advances in the west along the Mississippi River. Lee believed that a victory over the Army of the Potomac would force Lincoln to recall his troops from Mississippi. The Union president would need these soldiers to protect the North's capital from a victorious Army of Northern Virginia.

Such a recall of western Union forces would weaken Ulysses S. Grant's army, which now threatened Vicksburg, the last Confederate stronghold on the Mississippi River. With a reduced army, Grant would probably not be able to capture the Mississippi city.

By invading the North, Lee hoped to have Ulysses S. Grant's army, at the time threatening to lay siege to Vicksburg, recalled to the North.

Life in the Army

outline was the word for camp life for both Union and Confederate troops. Combat was one of the few breaks in this routine.

A soldier's day started early at 5:00 A.M. in the summer and 6:00 A.M. in the winter. Drums or bugles sounded reveille, and the soldier had fifteen minutes to wash and dress before assembly and roll call. The infantry then went to breakfast, the cavalry to care for their horses.

Assignments to guard duty, kitchen work, and camp chores, as well as sick call, followed breakfast. Those not assigned to work parties spent the rest of the morning drilling. Dinner was served at noon. It was followed, as New York private Theodore Winthrop wrote, "by target practice, . . . drill, more . . . drill, and. . . . tent inspection."

At 5:45 P.M. came retreat, which was an inspection and a dress parade. Each soldier carefully checked to see that all his weapons and buckles were polished, his belt and other leather items shined, and his uniform brushed. At retreat, officers read out orders, messages from army command, and court-martial results. Then the troops went to supper.

After supper, a soldier who was not on guard or kitchen duty was free to talk, play cards, or join a baseball game. At 8:30 P.M. he had to report to a final assembly and roll call known as tattoo. A half hour later taps sounded, and each soldier had to be in bed with lights out.

Scenes from camp life include (above) drilling and (right) washing clothes. The excitement of the battlefield were in most cases a welcome relief from the boredom of camp life.

The situation in the Confederate west was desperate. Except for Vicksburg, Union forces had almost complete control of the Mississippi River. If Grant were able to take Vicksburg, the Confederate states west of the river would be cut off from those east of it. The Confederacy would be chopped in two.

Even as the Southern cabinet and Lee met, Grant and his army were closing in on Vicksburg. Confederate leaders knew that it was only a matter of days before the Federals would besiege the Mississippi city. Even though Vicksburg was heavily fortified, it could not hold out forever without help. A few days earlier President Davis and Confederate secretary of war James A. Seddon had asked Lee to send part of the Army of Northern Virginia to defend Vicksburg. Lee had rejected the idea.

Lee agreed with Davis and Seddon that matters in Mississippi were serious, but he disagreed that sending troops from the Army of Northern Virginia was the solution. First, he did not believe the troops could reach Vicksburg in time. Union soldiers had destroyed much of the railroad that connected the eastern and western Confederacy. As historian James M. McPherson notes, "It would take weeks . . . to travel nearly a thousand miles to Mississippi over the Confederacy's mangled railroads."

Second, Lee pointed out that splitting his command would weaken the Army of Northern Virginia. With a weakened army,

A scene from Grant's siege of Vicksburg shows Union and Confederate troops facing off in a crater formed by an exploding mine.

he might not be able to defend Richmond against any future attacks by the Army of the Potomac.

For Lee, it became "a question between Virginia and Mississippi." And Lee was first and foremost a Virginian. In 1861 he had resigned from the U.S. Army saying, "I devote myself to the service of my native state, in whose behalf alone will I ever again draw my sword." Additionally, as historian Bruce Catton points out:

> To give up Virginia would be to give up Richmond, national capital, symbol of nationhood, source too of essential munitions and manufactures; loss here would probably mean speedy loss of the war itself.

To Gain European Recognition of the Confederacy

Lee also hoped that a Southern victory on Union soil would encourage England and France to recognize the Confederacy as an independent nation. Europe might then agree to send money and weapons to the South. Similar aid from France during the Revolutionary War had helped the rebellious colonies win that conflict.

The Confederacy had sought foreign recognition since its beginnings in 1861. Although France seemed willing to recognize the South if England did so first, England had remained neutral. British prime minister Viscount Palmerston wrote that the Confederacy would not be "a bit more independent for our saying so unless we followed up our Declaration by taking Part with them in the war." England had no intention of getting involved in the fighting between North and South, and the prime minister ended by saying that England "must know that their [the Confederacy's] separate independence is a truth and a fact." In other words, the South had to win the war or at least be on its way to winning before it could gain British recognition.

Lee was certain that a successful invasion of the North would satisfy Viscount Palmerston's requirements and earn the Confederacy both English and French recognition. As Union general Abner Doubleday later wrote in his history of Gettysburg:

> The agents of the Confederate Government stated . . . that if General Lee could establish his army firmly on Northern soil England would at once acknowledge the independence of the South; in which case ample loans could . . . be obtained . . . [and] a foreign alliance might be formed, and perhaps a fleet furnished to reopen the Southern ports.

Similar reports came from John Slidell, the Confederate representative to France.

Jefferson Davis

Jefferson Davis, the only president of the Confederacy, was born in 1808 in Kentucky. (Abraham Lincoln would be born in the same state a year later.) Davis graduated from West Point in 1828 and served in the U.S. Army until 1835 when he resigned to become a plantation owner in Mississippi. In 1848 he led a Mississippi unit in the Mexican War.

Davis served in both the U.S. House of Representatives and the Senate. He was also secretary of war under President Franklin Pierce (1853–1857). In January 1861 Davis left the U.S. Senate and gave up his U.S. citizenship when Mississippi seceded from the Union.

Davis became president of the Confederacy in February 1861 and personally ran the Confederate army. However, Davis was not an easy man to work with; he dismissed six secretaries of war and feuded with several of his top generals. Many members of the Confederate Congress believed that the president acted too much like a dictator. One opponent described Davis as "ambitious as Lucifer [the devil] and cold as a lizard."

When the Confederacy fell in 1865, Davis was captured and spent two years in prison facing charges of treason. However, he was never tried and eventually returned to Mississippi. Davis wrote *The Rise and Fall of the Confederate Government* before his death in 1889. He never tried to restore his U.S. citizenship.

Jefferson Davis led the South during the Civil War.

Looking to the Union Peace Movement

Finally, a Confederate invasion of and victory in the North might strengthen the growing peace movement in the North. These antiwar Northerners called themselves Peace Democrats; their enemies called them Copperheads. The latter name came from a venomous snake common to the eastern and central United States. In the nineteenth century, people thought copperhead snakes were tricky and struck without warning.

The Peace Democrats were outspoken in their opposition to the war. Many were disgusted by the huge loss of life. Others believed that the Union could easily survive without the South, and some were Southern sympathizers.

The Copperheads wanted immediate peace, even if it meant granting independence to the Confederacy. Peace Democrat Clement L. Vallandigham, who was running for governor of Ohio, called on the federal government to "stop the fighting. Make an armistice [truce]. Withdraw your army from the secessionist states."

Some Confederate spies in the Union claimed that a victory by Lee and his army in the North might lead the Copperheads to riot. These riots, if they spread, would tie up troops needed to fight the invading Confederates.

Reports of Copperhead activities and speeches convinced "the Davis Government . . . of the disaffection [unhappiness] there [the North]," noted Doubleday. As Lee told Davis:

> We should neglect no honorable means of dividing and weakening our enemies. . . . The most effectual mode of accomplishing this object . . . is to give all encouragement . . . to the rising peace party of the North.

Opposition to Lee's Plan

Lee was very persuasive and his various points impressed Jefferson Davis and most of the president's cabinet. Writer Shelby Foote observes, "They were not only persuaded by his logic; they were awed by his presence, his aura of invincibility."

However, one cabinet member refused to accept Lee's logic or be swayed by the general's personality. Confederate postmaster general John H. Reagan believed the invasion was a bad idea.

Reagan, who was from Texas, was the only person at the meeting whose home was west of the Mississippi. He believed that the fall of Vicksburg would be a disaster—cutting the Confederacy in two and resulting in certain defeat. To prevent

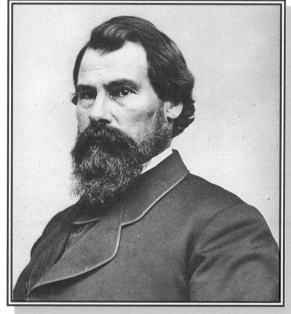

Confederate postmaster general John H. Reagan's refusal to agree to Lee's planned invasion of the North would prove prophetic.

such a catastrophe, the postmaster general wanted Lee to send reinforcements to Vicksburg immediately.

Further, Reagan vigorously disagreed with Lee on the benefits of invading Pennsylvania. The postmaster general thought that if Lee won a Northern battle, the antiwar and prowar factions in the Union would unite to oppose a common threat.

Reagan was unable to sway Davis or the rest of the cabinet, and it approved Lee's plan by a vote of five to one. Reagan was so convinced that the invasion would lead to disaster that he talked Davis into reconvening the cabinet and reopening the discussion. However, after long hours of debate, the second vote confirmed the first. On May 17, 1863, Lee joined the Army of Northern Virginia and began preparing for his invasion of the North.

CHAPTER TWO

Lee Advances North: To Find and Fight the Enemy

By the late spring of 1863, both the Army of Northern Virginia and the Army of the Potomac were on an equal footing. Both had about the same number of war-hardened veterans and weapons. The Northern army was the larger of the two but not by enough to give it much advantage in combat.

The advantage that the Army of Northern Virginia had enjoyed over its opponent for the past year had been its leadership. Lee had outgeneraled every one of the Army of the Potomac commanders he had confronted. In each fight between the two armies, it had been the Northern commanding general who had made the costly mistakes and lost the battle. In the Battle of Gettysburg, Lee would make the fatal errors.

On the Banks of the Rappahannock

As soon as Lee rejoined the Army of Northern Virginia after his Richmond trip, he began preparing for the invasion of the North. His troops were camped at Fredericksburg, Virginia, on the banks of the Rappahannock River about halfway between Richmond and Washington, D.C.

Lee had two immediate problems. First, he had to make his invasion preparations in sight of the Army of the Potomac, which sat on the opposite shore of the Rappahannock. The Federals had retreated and dug in there after the Battle of Chancellorsville two weeks before.

As Lee pointed out to his superiors at Confederate army headquarters in Richmond, the Union army had fortified its position so

While thought by many to be the first modern war, the primitive conditions found in the military camps of both sides in the Civil War were not much better than those found in the camps of Alexander the Great centuries earlier.

well that Lee saw no way of successfully attacking it. "The position occupied by the enemy opposite Fredericksburg," he wrote, "[is] one in which he [the enemy] could not be attacked to advantage."

Consequently, Lee tightened security. He increased the number of guard patrols around the Confederate camp, in part to cut down on the number of deserters. Deserters not only reduced the ranks of the Army of Northern Virginia, but some sought shelter with the Federals. These former Confederate soldiers could well pass valuable information about Lee's plans to Hooker.

Lee also forbade his men to talk to the Union soldiers across the river. Confederate and Union enlisted men often swapped stories, advice, and gossip across the no-man's-land between armies. It was one way to relieve the long spells of boredom between combat. None of this friendliness kept these men from trying to kill each other during battle.

How the Armies Were Organized

The infantry of both the Army of Northern Virginia and the Army of the Potomac had the same general organization. The basic unit was the company, then the regiment, followed by the brigade, the division, and finally, the corps.

Generally ten companies formed a regiment, and four or five regiments made up a brigade. In the Army of Northern Virginia, four or five brigades composed a division, while in the Army of the Potomac, two or three did. In both armies, three divisions was the normal strength of a corps. The Southern army had three corps, and the Northern force had seven.

The difference in the number of corps between the two armies did not mean that the Army of the Potomac was twice the size of the Army of Northern Virginia because Confederate army units tended to have more soldiers than Union units. For instance, the average Southern company had 4 officers and from 90 to 120 enlisted men. A Northern company had only 3 officers and from 80 to 95 enlisted men.

At Gettysburg, the Northern army was only 25 percent larger than the Southern army.

In addition to the infantry corps, each army had a separate cavalry section, which was either a division or a corps depending upon its size. In the Confederate army, artillery units were assigned to each infantry division; in the Federal army, part of the artillery was distributed between corps, and the remainder was collected together in an artillery reserve.

Overall, the Army of Northern Virginia's organization was superior to that of the Army of the Potomac. Lee only had four officers immediately below him, and he could check with them more quickly than Northern commander Meade could consult with his nine subordinates. Lee could move one-third of his infantry to anywhere on the field with an order to a single corps. On the other hand, Meade would have to contact two, perhaps three, of his corps to move the same proportion of his force.

The Army of the Potomac is drilled in its winter quarters. The Union army's organization hampered its maneuverability on the battlefield.

Supplies and Reinforcements

Lee also had to bring the Army of Northern Virginia up to full fighting strength after its large losses at the Battle of Chancellorsville. Lee pulled in reinforcements from Confederate units all over Virginia. Men poured in, as did weapons, equipment, food, and wagons with horses and mules to draw them.

Lee's biggest headache was how to deal with the death of General Stonewall Jackson. Jackson had been Lee's most trusted officer, a man whom Lee depended on to carry out his orders with imagination and boldness. "I know not how to replace him," Lee said.

Lee decided that he could probably work around his loss of Jackson by reorganizing the Army of Northern Virginia. Accordingly, he divided his infantry into three corps. First Corps was commanded by General James Longstreet, Second Corps by General

An artist depicts the last time that Lee gave orders to Thomas "Stonewall" Jackson before his death at Chancellorsville. Jackson received his nickname at the First Battle of Bull Run when he steadfastly led his troops even though the battle seemed to be going against the Southerners.

James Longstreet

James Longstreet, born in 1821 in South Carolina, graduated from West Point in 1842 and was wounded in the 1848 Mexican War. He reached the rank of major before resigning from the U.S. Army in June 1861 to become a general in the Confederate army.

Within a year, he was commanding the Army of Northern Virginia's First Corps. He proved to be a capable corps commander and played an important role in winning battles in Virginia in 1862 and 1863.

After Gettysburg, Longstreet spent the fall of 1863 in Tennessee, where he helped Confederate forces win the Battle of Chickamauga. He then returned to lead the Army of Northern Virginia's First Corps until the surrender at Appomattox in April 1865.

After the war, Longstreet supported Reconstruction, at one time leading a band of black soldiers against rioting whites in New Orleans. He became a Republican like his old friend and West Point classmate Ulysses S. Grant and served as minister to Turkey while Grant was president.

Longstreet's politics angered many former Confederates, and they did much to smear

General James Longstreet, also nicknamed the "Warhorse," played a pivotal role in the Battle of Gettysburg.

his name, including blaming him for the defeat at Gettysburg. Before his death in 1904, Longstreet set the record straight in his book *From Manassas to Appomattox.*

Richard S. Ewell, and Third Corps by General A. P. Hill. Most of the men who had served under Jackson were now in the Second Corps under Ewell, who had been Jackson's second in command.

Lee and Longstreet

Of the three corps commanders, only James Longstreet had served in that position before. Longstreet, whose troops called him "Old Pete," was Lee's most experienced lieutenant. He had won Lee's admiration for his capable soldiering in the past; Lee felt he could count on Old Pete, and called him "my old warhorse."

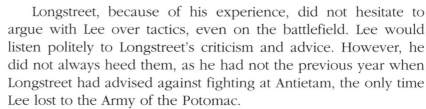

Deserters North and South

Desertion was a problem throughout the entire war for both the North and the South, particularly before a major campaign. It was easy for soldiers to walk away from camp, and it was impossible to track them down, particularly since the number of deserters ran into the thousands on both sides. Writer Jack Coggins notes:

> As accustomed as we are to the rules, regulations, and red tape of soldiering in the twentieth century, it seems incredible that thousands of men of both armies should wander off. . . . [Yet] it is safe to estimate that, given twenty thousand infantry to start with, a general would be lucky if, after two or three weeks . . . , he would be able to put sixteen thousand into the line of battle.

Indeed, one Union general estimated that some 8,000 men and 250 officers deserted from the Army of the Potomac's First Corps before the Battle of Antietam.

Southern soldiers often left their units after a major battle and went home. These men believed that they had served the Confederacy. Now they were needed at home to harvest crops or to make money to feed their families.

Longstreet, because of his experience, did not hesitate to argue with Lee over tactics, even on the battlefield. Lee would listen politely to Longstreet's criticism and advice. However, he did not always heed them, as he had not the previous year when Longstreet had advised against fighting at Antietam, the only time Lee lost to the Army of the Potomac.

At Gettysburg, Lee would make the mistake of ignoring Longstreet's misgivings about fighting the Federals on this particular battlefield. It would be one of the mistakes that led to Lee and the Army of Northern Virginia's losing the battle.

Across the River

Meanwhile, on the opposite bank of the Rappahannock, Army of the Potomac commander Joseph "Fighting Joe" Hooker and his men watched as soldiers and supplies rolled into the Confederate camp. Hooker, whom Lee always called "Mr. F. J. Hooker," knew that the Army of Northern Virginia was preparing for a major campaign, but he had no idea what its goal was. Union intelligence concluded that Lee meant to move the Army of Northern Virginia west and then north so as to attack the Army of the Potomac's right rear.

Hooker could do little but wait. He did propose to Abraham Lincoln that the Army of the Potomac should attack Richmond if Lee moved out. Lincoln squashed this suggestion, saying that Hooker and his troops' target for now was the Army of Northern Virginia. If the Federal army could defeat, or even destroy, this major eastern Confederate army, they could clear the way to attack and take Richmond.

The March North Begins

By the end of May, the Army of Northern Virginia was ready. It now numbered seventy-five thousand troops, and beginning on June 3, Lee began sending units westward. For the moment, Lee left his Third Corps and its commander General Hill at Fredericksburg to discourage the Army of the Potomac from crossing the Rappahannock and either attacking the Southern army from the rear or from marching on Richmond.

Lee's planned route was an arc that would take the Army of Northern Virginia west to the Shenandoah Valley, then north along the Shenandoah into Maryland, and finally up into the Cumberland Valley and central Pennsylvania. During the Civil War, the broad, generally flat Shenandoah Valley served as a natural highway for both Southern and Northern troops moving into and out of Virginia.

Flamboyant Southern cavalry commander Jeb Stuart sits holding his famed plumed hat, one of the many symbols that made the man a popular emblem of superior Southern cleverness and audacity.

Skirmish at Brandy Station

The route to Pennsylvania first took Lee and his men to Brandy Station, Virginia. Waiting for Lee was the Army of Northern Virginia's cavalry division commanded by James E. B. "Jeb" Stuart.

Stuart was one of the best cavalry commanders on either side, and he was also one of the most colorful characters in the entire war. Thinking of himself as a swashbuckling hero of old, he wore a plumed hat and a cape and loved to take on bold adventures, particularly if the newspapers published stories about him.

Twice during battles, he and his command had ridden around the entire Army of the Potomac. These rides had served no practical purpose, but it had been good for Southern morale to hear and read about Confederate cavalry literally riding rings around the Federals.

Despite Stuart's dashing nature, he knew his job and generally did it well. In an age without airplanes or spy satellites, cavalry units were the only way generals could get fast, detailed reports on their enemy's movements. Army commanders also depended upon their mounted units to screen them from the spying eyes of enemy cavalry. Stuart and his men were excellent at both tasks.

Lee arrived at Brandy Station on June 9, just after Stuart's troops finished beating off a massed attack by Union cavalry. Hooker had dispatched Union troops to spy on Lee's army. Running into Stuart's cavalry division, the Union horsemen had attacked.

In the past, Northern mounted units had been second rate compared to their Southern counterparts, but at Brandy Station, the Federal cavalry showed that it was now a tough opponent. It took Stuart and his troopers most of the day to drive off the Union horse soldiers in what would turn out to be the largest cavalry battle of the Civil War.

Up the Shenandoah

Over the next few days, the Southern army moved west and then north into the Shenandoah Valley. Ewell's Second Corps led the way, followed by Longstreet's First Corps. The Third Corps remained at Fredericksburg.

On June 14, Ewell and his corps attacked and drove off the Union garrison at Winchester, Virginia, just a few miles south of the Maryland border. The next day the Second Corps crossed the Potomac and reentered Union territory. Except for a series of small skirmishes between Confederate and Union cavalry, Lee's army did no more fighting on its march into Pennsylvania. Indeed, the going was so easy that the soldiers joked "breakfast in Virginia, whiskey in Maryland, and supper in Pennsylvania."

Hooker, having received word that Ewell was at Winchester, had finally left the Fredericksburg area and moved north. The Union general still did not know what Lee's goal was so he moved his troops toward the Potomac River, keeping his army between the Confederates and Washington, D.C.

When the Army of the Potomac departed, Hill took his Third Corps west to join Lee and the rest of the army. Now, the Army of Northern Virginia stretched in a thin, one-hundred-mile-long line down the Shenandoah Valley.

In Pennsylvania

Lee made no attempt to pull the Army of Northern Virginia together when it reached Pennsylvania. Ewell's Second Corps reached Pennsylvania on June 24 and continued to move north, heading toward the state capital of Harrisburg. Lee, arriving soon after, set up his headquarters at Chambersburg, a few miles north of the Pennsylvania-Maryland state line.

Lee let his army spread out so that the various units could seek supplies over as large an area as possible. The Southern soldiers gathered food, medicine, horse equipment, and clothes from Pennsylvania towns and farms. They also took every healthy horse they found; the number of horses eventually totaled in the thousands.

Rebel troops cross the Potomac on their way to invade Maryland and Pennsylvania. (Left) Major General Richard Stoddert Ewell led the Second Corps in the Battle of Gettysburg. Ewell lost a leg in the early part of the Civil War and fought for nearly three years with one wooden leg.

Lee gave his troops strict orders not to steal and to pay for everything they took. However, the soldiers could only pay in Confederate money, which was almost worthless—even in the South. Further, Lee ordered his soldiers not to hurt the civilian population or their property: "We make war only upon armed men and . . . we cannot take vengeance for the wrongs our people have suffered without lowering ourselves in the eyes of all."

Not all of the Army of Northern Virginia followed these orders. General Jubal Early of the Second Corps burned down the iron foundry of Thaddeus Stevens, a U.S. congressman and famous abolitionist. Most Southerners, however, acted as did General John B. Gordon of the Second Corps:

I resolved to leave no ruins along the line of my march through Pennsylvania; no marks of a more enduring character [lasting nature] than the tracks of my soldiers along its [Pennsylvania's] superb pikes [roads].

One group of Pennsylvania citizens did not enjoy Lee's protection: African Americans. Confederates routinely rounded up black Pennsylvanians and shipped them south into slavery. Even though Lee personally detested slavery and wanted to see it ended, he turned a blind eye toward these mass human shipments. At least

Civil War Discipline

Discipline in both the Federal and Confederate armies was often harsh and cruel by modern standards. A soldier guilty of a minor offense, such as drunkenness, stealing from fellow soldiers, or sitting while on guard duty, might have to wear a cannonball chained to his leg or to march around the camp with a pack filled with rocks. Punishments lasted hours, sometimes a full day.

In artillery units, a common punishment was to tie a spread-eagled soldier to a wheel that was then lashed onto a gun carriage. The carriage was driven over rough ground to cause the bound man a great deal of pain. Those who cried out in pain were gagged by having a stick tied into their mouths.

More serious crimes, which included mutiny, rape, or desertion, could send the offender to military prison. Such crimes were sometimes punished by branding the guilty soldier on the forehead with, for example, a *D* for deserter or a *C* for coward.

A soldier could also be executed for murder, treason, and desertion. During the war, several hundred Union and Confederate soldiers were executed, most by firing squad for desertion.

Many soldiers resented these punishments, particularly the executions, which they were forced to watch. However, others believed these methods, as one Union private wrote, "served their purpose. . . . The times were cruel, and men had been hardened to bear the suffering of other men without wincing."

one Confederate, William S. Christian, could not bring himself to send blacks south: "We took a lot of Negroes yesterday. . . . My humanity revolted at taking the poor devils from their homes. They were so scared that I turned them all loose."

Fighting Joe Hooker Refuses the Fight

As Lee marched north, panic spread in the Union, particularly in central Pennsylvania where no Federal troops were stationed. Charles Coffin, a reporter for the *Boston Journal*, described the following scene in Harrisburg, capital of Pennsylvania and forty miles northeast of Gettysburg:

> Harrisburg was a Bedlam [madhouse]. . . . The railroad stations were crowded with an excited people—men, women, and children—with trunks, boxes, bundles; packages tied up in bed-blankets and quilts; mountains of luggage—tumbling it into the [railroad] cars, rushing here and there in a frantic manner; shouting, screaming, as if the Rebels were about to dash into the town and lay it in ashes.

By June 21 Union cavalry had reported that the Army of Northern Virginia was strung out along the length of the Shenandoah Valley. Lincoln suggested to Hooker, who had been moving the Army of the Potomac slowly north and west, that the Union commander attack Lee's force and cut it in two. Hooker refused, saying that he could not attack because he was sure that he was outnumbered. He requested reinforcements but complained that the replacements were poor soldiers even though they were all veterans. Instead of attacking the spread-out seventy-five thousand Confederates with his now ninety-five thousand soldiers, Hooker continued his slow advance until he reached Frederick in western Maryland.

Everyone from Lincoln on down was fed up with Fighting Joe and his lack of fighting. The *Chicago Tribune* wrote:

> Under the leadership of "Fighting Joe Hooker" the glorious Army of the Potomac is becoming more slow in its movements, . . . less confident of itself, . . . and less an honor to the country than any army we have yet raised.

On June 28 Lincoln relieved Hooker of command of the Army of the Potomac. The army's new commander was General George G. Meade, who until then had been leading the Army of the Potomac's Fifth Corps. Meade was the fifth general to lead the Army of the Potomac in the past year.

Stuart and the Cavalry Ride Out

While the Union army pursued Lee and the Army of Northern Virginia, the Southern commander made his first serious mistake of the campaign. He ordered Jeb Stuart to move his cavalry by the most direct route north to join up with Ewell's Second Corps.

As was usual in a campaign, Stuart and his horse soldiers were also to make fast raids against the Union army whenever possible. Furthermore, they were to capture whatever supplies they could.

Normally such operations might take the cavalry far from the main body of the Southern army, but this time Lee wanted his horse troops to stay close. The Army of Northern Virginia was marching through foreign and hostile territory, and the Southern commander needed all the information that his mounted spies could provide. Lee wanted Stuart and his men to ride between the two armies and never lose contact with the Confederate force.

However, the orders were not well written. Stuart, always on the lookout for a new adventure, read them as permission to ride once more around the entire Army of the Potomac. He thus placed the Federals between his cavalry and Lee.

Stuart and his troops left Lee on June 24. They made their end run of the Union army without any trouble, but they found circling it impossible. The Federal army was moving just fast enough that every time Stuart turned to ride back to the Army of Northern Virginia, he found his way blocked by a column of bluecoated soldiers. Lee would not see his cavalry again until the second day of the Battle of Gettysburg one week later.

An Army Without Eyes

By sending his cavalry off, Lee created a serious problem. Without his mounted eyes, the Southern commander had no idea where the Army of the Potomac was and what it was doing. Nor could he hide his troop movements from Federal cavalry.

Lee knew all too well the dangers involved in losing one's cavalry. Six weeks before at Chancellorsville, Hooker had lost the battle because he had sent his cavalry off. Stonewall Jackson had then been able to launch a successful surprise attack on the Army of the Potomac's rear. The same sort of surprise could well await Lee and the Army of Northern Virginia.

And indeed, Lee was surprised on June 28. A spy sent out by Longstreet told the Southern commander that the Army of the Potomac, which Lee still thought to be in Virginia, was actually at Frederick in western Maryland, only forty miles south of Lee's headquarters at Chambersburg. The Army of Northern Virginia was still scattered over much of central Pennsylvania, and Lee immediately ordered all his units to fall back to the Chambersburg area.

Without his cavalry to spy out the Army of the Potomac's location, Lee had to wait until the Federal army found him or some accident brought the two forces together. Historian Bruce Catton writes, "Lee . . . [was] condemned at last to fight a battle in which he could not maneuver." For the first time in his year-long campaign against the Army of the Potomac, he had lost the initiative.

Meade Takes Command

Longstreet's spy also told Lee that General Hooker had been relieved of his post and that General Meade was the new Northern commander. Although many of Lee's officers thought that Meade would prove to be as poor a leader as Hooker, Lee did not agree. "General Meade will commit no blunder on my front, and if I make one he will make haste to take advantage of it."

At the time, Meade was a very busy man. Although he had led the Army of the Potomac's Fifth Corps, he knew little about the detailed workings of the whole army. Normally, the new commander would have taken several weeks to study these details, but Lee was already in Pennsylvania. Meade had to counter the threat posed by the Confederate invasion now, not weeks from now.

Meade's first act was to make a quick survey of the army that he had inherited. He found that the Army of the Potomac had a strong core of battle-hardened veterans and that it was ready to fight. "Supplies were plentiful and morale was good," writes historian Albert Nofi.

Morale was good, too, because the Army of the Potomac now marched on home ground. Unlike in Virginia, where they were hated as invaders, here they were cheered as heroes. As Union lieutenant Jesse Young wrote, "The hearty greeting given to the soldiers . . . gladdened the army. . . . The Stars and Stripes were everywhere . . . ; men, women, and children vied [competed] with one another in their exhibitions of loyalty." As one Union soldier said, "We felt some doubt about whether it was ever going to be our fortune to win a victory in Virginia, but no one admitted the possibility of a defeat north of the Potomac."

Meade had seven infantry corps under his command. However, Union units tended to be smaller than Confederate ones, and he did not have twice as many soldiers as Lee but rather about 25 percent more. General John F. Reynolds led First Corps; General Winfield Scott Hancock commanded Second Corps; General Daniel E. Sickles, Third Corps; General George Sykes, Fifth Corps; General John Sedgewick, Sixth Corps; General Oliver O. Howard, Eleventh Corps; and General Henry W. Slocum, Twelfth Corps.

Meade Heads for Battle

Compared to Hooker who was known for his boasting, heavy drinking, and vicious fights with superiors, Meade was quiet and colorless. However, he had an excellent combat record, and

George G. Meade

George Gordon Meade was born in 1815 of American parents living in Spain but originally from Pennsylvania. Meade graduated from West Point in 1835, but he left the army after a year to become a civil engineer. Returning to the army in 1842, he served in the 1848 Mexican War and was a captain in the engineers when the Civil War broke out.

Meade was given command of Pennsylvania volunteers and promoted to general. He proved to be a good battlefield commander and led his troops well even at major Union defeats, such as Fredericksburg and Chancellorsville.

After Gettysburg he remained in command of the Army of the Potomac until the end of the war. However, he was overshadowed by General in Chief Ulysses S. Grant, who set up his headquarters with Meade and the Army of the Potomac in 1864.

Grant had originally intended to replace Meade as commander of the Army of the Potomac, but Meade so impressed Grant on their first meeting that he declined Meade's offer to step down if it would help the war effort. Grant wrote that Meade was one of the

George Meade replaced Joseph Hooker as the commander of the Army of the Potomac.

finest officers "for large commands I have come in contact with."

Meade remained in the army after the end of the war. He served in the South during Reconstruction and died in 1872.

Pennsylvania was his home. "Meade will fight well on his own dung hill," Lincoln said.

Meade immediately marched the Army of the Potomac north to Taneytown, Maryland, just south of the Pennsylvania state line and about twelve miles from Gettysburg. He ordered his cavalry to spread out into Pennsylvania and find the Army of Northern Virginia. Some Federal mounted soldiers reached Gettysburg on June 30.

Meanwhile, at nearby Pipe Creek, Meade located an area that could be easily defended if and when Lee and the Army of Northern Virginia attacked. He set his men to digging trenches along the creek's banks.

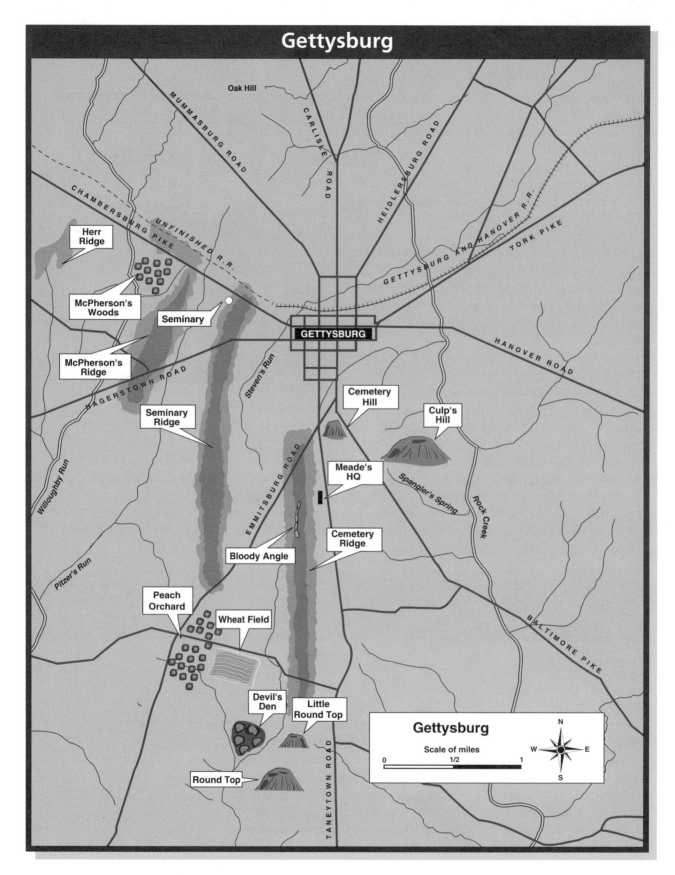

Gettysburg

Oak Hill

MUMMASBURG ROAD

CARLISKE ROAD

HEIDLERSBURG ROAD

GETTYSBURG AND HANOVER R.R.

YORK PIKE

CHAMBERSBURG PIKE

UNFINISHED R.R.

Herr Ridge

McPherson's Woods

Seminary

McPherson's Ridge

HAGERSTOWN ROAD

HANOVER ROAD

GETTYSBURG

Steven's Run

Seminary Ridge

Cemetery Hill

Culp's Hill

Spangler's Spring

Rock Creek

Willoughby Run

EMMITSBURG ROAD

Meade's HQ

Bloody Angle

Cemetery Ridge

Pitzer's Run

Peach Orchard

Wheat Field

BALTIMORE PIKE

Devil's Den

Little Round Top

Round Top

TANEYTOWN ROAD

Gettysburg

Scale of miles

0   1/2   1

N
W   E
S

The Battle Begins

Even as Union soldiers dug trenches along Pipe Creek, the battle that both Lee and Meade expected began when Confederates and Federals collided at Gettysburg. On June 30 a unit of the Army of Northern Virginia's Third Corps went looking for shoes reportedly stored at Gettysburg. There, they ran into Army of the Potomac cavalry under the command of General John Buford. The Confederates retreated, and the Federals sent word of the encounter to Pipe Creek.

The next morning, the Confederates returned. The attackers were General Henry Heth and his division, also part of Third Corps. Heth and his men were met, in the words of Confederate general Fitzhugh Lee, by a "few sputtering shots, which . . . told him [Heth] that . . . Buford's . . . cavalry were blocking the way."

It was July 1, 1863, day one of the Battle of Gettysburg.

CHAPTER THREE

Day One: We Are Met on a Great Battlefield

It was a warm, humid Wednesday that July 1, 1863, when the Army of Northern Virginia and the Army of the Potomac finally met on the battlefield of Gettysburg. As Confederate general and division commander Henry Heth and his men approached Gettysburg, it was only an hour after dawn. At this time of year, the days were still long and the nights short in central Pennsylvania. The sun had risen just a little after 4:30 A.M. and would not set until 7:30 P.M. The troops faced long days of battle and short nights of rest.

Heth Goes for His Shoes

The previous evening, Heth had told his commanding officer, General and Third Corps commander A. P. Hill, that he believed Gettysburg was defended by only a few soldiers. The division commander very much wanted to run the Union defenders off and get to the supply of shoes rumored to be in the town. Shoes were in short supply in the Confederate army, and plenty of Heth's men were either barefoot or wearing shoes that were falling apart. When Heth asked if Hill had any objection to his going after those shoes, Hill replied, "None in the world."

Hill gave his permission because both he and Heth thought that the Army of the Potomac was camped at Taneytown, Maryland. Both Confederate generals believed that the soldiers at Gettysburg were only local volunteers, not regular army. As Heth later said, "I knew they would run as soon as we appeared."

The Third Corps commander might not have been so ready to say yes if he had known that Union general John F. Reynolds's

First Corps was just six miles south of town and not far behind it were General Oliver O. Howard's Eleventh Corps, General Daniel E. Sickles's Third Corps, and General Henry W. Slocum's Twelfth Corps.

Jeb Stuart's cavalry that should have provided this information to Hill was still missing. According to historian Bruce Catton the reckless Stuart "had slipped the leash." Thus, when Heth launched his Gettysburg attack, he thought that he and his soldiers were only in for a small skirmish, not a full-fledged battle.

Buford Waits at Gettysburg

The defenders at Gettysburg were a far cry from local volunteers. They were two full brigades of Army of the Potomac cavalry, totaling about three thousand troopers. Heth's division with seventy-five hundred men still outnumbered the Federals, but the latter carried the new Spencer repeating rifles that allowed them to fire five times more shots a minute than the Southern soldiers could shoot with their more commonplace muzzle-loading guns.

Gettysburg would be the last battle for Union general John F. Reynolds, who would die from a sharpshooter's bullet to the head one hour after taking the battlefield.

Commanding the Union horse soldiers was a talented cavalry leader, General John Buford. As writer Shelby Foote notes, "Buford was all business and hard action. . . . He drove himself as mercilessly as he did his men."

After the Confederate retreat the previous day, the Union cavalry chief notified General John F. Reynolds, whose First Corps was the Federal infantry unit closest to Gettysburg. Buford asked Reynolds to send reinforcements and to inform Meade at Taneytown of the Confederate attackers. He added that he thought Gettysburg was the place to fight a major battle.

Then Buford prepared for the Southern soldiers' return. He placed one of his brigades just west of town to cover the road down which the Confederates would most likely come. His other brigade guarded the northern approach.

Buford told his men to expect a large attack. "They [the Confederates] will come booming—skirmishers [soldiers] three-deep," he said. "You will have to fight like the devil until support arrives." When Heth's division appeared from the west, marching three deep as Buford had predicted, the Union soldiers opened fire.

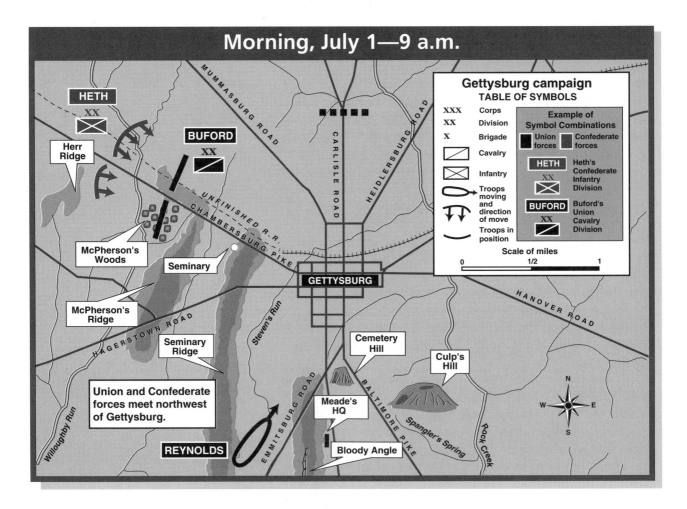

Morning, July 1—9 a.m.

Gettysburg campaign
TABLE OF SYMBOLS

XXX	Corps
XX	Division
X	Brigade
	Cavalry
	Infantry
	Troops moving and direction of move
	Troops in position

Example of Symbol Combinations

Union forces / Confederate forces

HETH — Heth's Confederate Infantry Division

BUFORD — Buford's Union Cavalry Division

Scale of miles
0   1/2   1

The First Shots Are Fired

The fighting was slow at first, with the Confederates advancing cautiously, but as the morning wore on, Heth and his troops attacked more fiercely. They forced the Federals to fall back to McPherson's Ridge, about a mile west of Gettysburg and the first of the many important high grounds the Union army would hold during the battle.

Buford's men were now in a good position, stretched in a line along the ridge, which forced the Confederates to attack uphill. Uphill assaults are difficult because the attacking troops have to charge up a slope in the face of rifle fire.

It was now 10:00 A.M., and the first Union infantry finally arrived. Reynolds and one of his First Corps divisions headed for the fighting, battle flags waving and fife and drum corps playing a popular song of the day, "The Campbells Are Coming." And come the reinforcements did, just in time. By now, Buford's men were exhausted from over five hours of fighting in the mounting humid heat of the July day.

Reynolds agreed with Buford about Gettysburg. He too saw

it as an excellent spot to fight a major battle. There was plenty of high ground to which the Union troops could retreat if need be.

Reynolds sent messages to the other nearby Army of the Potomac corps requesting their help. He then wrote a quick note to Meade, telling the commanding general that "I will fight them [the Confederates] inch by inch, and if driven into the town I will barricade [block] the streets and hold them as long as possible."

The Federals Hold McPherson's Ridge

Even with the addition of the thirty-eight hundred men from Reynolds's corps, the fight was far from over, and the Federals were still slightly outnumbered. Heth's troops continued to attack and almost succeeded in overpowering first the right and then the left flanks, or ends, of the Federal line.

However, the bluecoated defenders beat back the Southern attack. In part this was due to the Union's Iron Brigade. The Iron Brigade, made up of midwestern units, was known for its hard fighting and distinctive black hats. These hats let the Confederates finally know whom they faced. One Southern soldier yelled out, "There are those   black-hatted fellows again! 'Taint no militia [local volunteers]! It's the Army of the Potomac!"

During the height of combat, a Confederate sharpshooter caught Reynolds in his sights and shot the Union general dead. The fatal rifle ball slammed into Reynolds just behind the right ear, killing him instantly. He had been at Gettysburg less than an hour.

General Abner Doubleday immediately took charge of the Union force and continued the fight. General Oliver O. Howard and Eleventh Corps, along with the remainder of First Corps, arrived about a half hour later, and Howard took over from Doubleday. The morning fighting came to a close with the Federals driving Heth's last men from McPherson's Ridge.

Union soldiers won the first engagement at Gettysburg and wiped out almost one quarter of the attacking force. The defenders had captured several hundred Confederates. The prisoners included one general, James J. Archer, the highest ranking of Lee's officers captured to date. But the battle was only beginning.

The Confederates Attack Again

The Union triumph was short-lived. As Howard stood looking over the field of battle, artillery shells began exploding right behind the center of the Union line. Because the shells fell with such precision, at least one Federal officer thought his own shells were falling short. But they were Confederate shells and marked the arrival of Ewell's Second Corps from the north.

Heth had sent word back to Hill of his fight with the Army of the Potomac, and Hill, without consulting Lee, dispatched the rest

(Top) These Confederate soldiers were taken prisoner at Gettysburg. (Right) The Wheat Field at Gettysburg where John Reynolds was shot to death. The famous Civil War photographer Matthew Brady is standing in the right-hand corner.

of his Third Corps to back up Heth. The Third Corps leader then sent a note to Ewell telling the Second Corps commander of Third Corps's destination. Ewell, who was on the road, returning from Harrisburg, decided that he and his men should join the Confederates at Gettysburg.

Hill himself took no active part in the day's fighting. He had become mysteriously ill the night before and could not even climb onto his horse the next morning.

To meet Ewell's approaching Second Corps, Howard moved his Eleventh Corps. He placed his men in a line along a shallow valley just north of the town. At a right angle to Eleventh Corps was Doubleday's First Corps, which stretched in a very long line along McPherson's Ridge. First Corps's left flank continued to fight off occasional attacks from Heth's soldiers.

As Howard waited for the Second Corps's attack, he sent messages to the Union commanders of Third Corps and Twelfth Corps telling them to hurry up. He wanted their troops desperately. Howard and Doubleday together had nineteen thousand Federals with which to fight twenty-five thousand Confederates.

Lee Heads for Gettysburg

Lee learned about the fighting at Gettysburg in the morning when he was out riding east of his headquarters at Chambersburg. In the distance, he heard the dull rumble of the far-off Northern and Southern artillery. The guns would be heard as far away as Pittsburgh, 150 miles west of Gettysburg.

Lee knew that the noise had to be coming from Gettysburg because Hill had told him about Heth's raid on the Pennsylvania town. He also knew that he was hearing the sounds of a serious battle, not a small raiding skirmish. The firing of the guns was lasting too long.

Lee was not happy with the possibility of a major battle having started at Gettysburg. His army was still spread out, and as he told his staff, without Stuart's cavalry he did not know "what we have in front of us here. It may be the whole Federal army, or it may be only a detachment." To get more information, Lee himself rode east to Gettysburg.

Meade Reacts

At Taneytown, Meade was still laying out his trenches at Pipe Creek. Unlike Lee, the Northern commander could not hear the boom of artillery; the rolling hills between the two towns apparently soaked up the noise of war. A reporter for the *New York Times*, who had just come from Gettysburg, told Meade the details of the morning's fighting and of the death of Reynolds. The

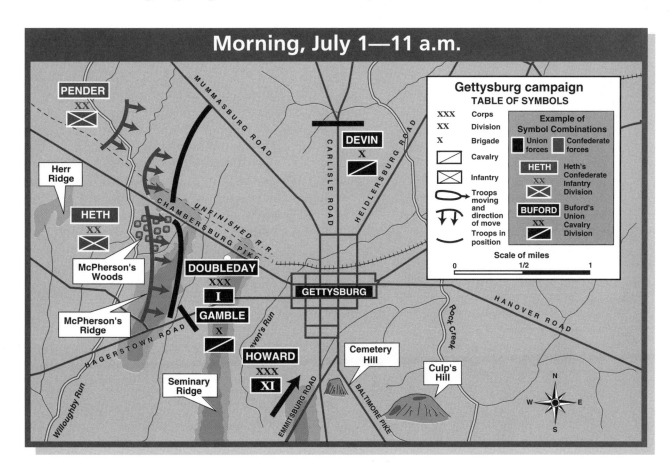

news left Meade wondering whether to send the whole Army of the Potomac to the escalating battle.

Like Lee, Meade decided that he needed more information; he instructed his Second Corps commander, General Winfield Scott Hancock, to go to Gettysburg. Hancock was to take command of the Union troops there and then look over the battlefield. "If you think the ground and position there a better one to fight a battle [than Pipe Creek] . . . ," went his orders, "you will so advise the General [Meade], and he will order all the troops up."

Hancock's being sent to take command from Howard, who was the senior of the two officers, showed Meade's confidence in the Second Corps leader's judgment and abilities. Hancock was indeed a very capable soldier, whose combat record had earned him the nickname "Superb." He was popular with the enlisted men, and just the sight of Hancock striding, head up, through even the fiercest firefight, always kept his men's morale high.

General Winfield Scott Hancock took over Reynolds's command, reforming the shattered corps and choosing to take a stand at Cemetery Hill, a position he would hold for the rest of the battle.

The Fighting Continues

While Lee was approaching Gettysburg from the west and Hancock was approaching from the south, the battle had heated up again. Confederate General Robert E. Rodes's division, part of Ewell's Second Corps, had launched an attack against both First and Eleventh Corps lines. Around 2:30 P.M., Rodes's artillery started shelling the center of First Corps and forced the Union soldiers to pull back. This opened a large hole in Doubleday's line.

Rodes had never commanded a division in battle before, and his more practiced corps commander was still some miles up the road riding behind another Second Corps division. Rodes was inexperienced and managed the Confederate advance poorly. His attack against First Corps was thrown back by the Union defenders. In a few minutes at the height of the fighting, 30 percent of the attackers were either killed or wounded when they walked directly into the massed murderous fire of the Union soldiers. Many of the remaining Southern soldiers were captured.

Eleventh Corps was also holding its own, and after an hour of fighting, Rodes's division had gained little. Then, the Confederate hammer fell.

Winfield Scott Hancock

Winfield Scott Hancock was born in 1824 in Pennsylvania and graduated from West Point in 1844. He was in the infantry during the 1848 Mexican War and was a captain in the quartermaster corps when the Civil War began.

In 1861 Hancock was in California. Before heading east, he gave a dinner party for several officers who were resigning to join the Confederacy. Among them was Lewis Armistead, who became a Confederate general and who died attacking Hancock's unit on the third day at Gettysburg.

Hancock was transferred to the Army of the Potomac in September 1862. He was placed in charge of a brigade of volunteers and promoted to general. He proved to be a dynamic and forceful combat leader, rising within a few months to leadership of Second Corps.

Hancock was wounded at Gettysburg when a bullet hit his saddle, driving wooden splinters and a saddle nail into his leg. After a long recovery, Hancock returned to active duty and fought under Grant in Virginia until his wound reopened in late 1864. He spent the remainder of the war in recruiting drives.

After the war, Hancock did Reconstruction duty in the South. In 1880 he was the Democratic candidate for president but lost to James Garfield. Hancock was still on active duty when he died in 1886.

The Confederates Strike Hard

In the north General Jubal Early's division, part of Ewell's Second Corps struck hard at Eleventh Corps. At almost the same time, in the west, a second division of Hill's Third Corps arrived and joined Heth's division to hit the still-split First Corps line.

The Confederates slammed so hard into the Union defenders that the latter reeled back in shock. Both First and Eleventh Corps backed into the town, where for the next hour, both sides fought a confused street-by-street battle. Around 4:30 P.M., the Federals pulled completely free of the town, leaving some twenty-five hundred prisoners in Confederate hands.

The Union retreat stopped at the top of Cemetery Hill, which was about a half mile south of the town square and which held the local graveyard. There, over one hundred feet above the ground, the bluecoated soldiers started digging trenches among the tombstones from which to fight off Confederate attackers.

Lee Surveys the Battle

Lee reached Gettysburg before Hancock. The afternoon battle was in full swing, and at first, Lee seriously thought of pulling his troops out of the battle. Without his still missing cavalry, the

Southern commander had no idea how many Federals fought his soldiers. He knew that only four of his army's nine divisions had reached Gettysburg. With less than half of his troops present, he was reluctant to stay and fight. As he told Heth, who had ridden up for orders, "I am not prepared to bring on a general engagement [battle] today."

However, as the Union troops began falling back in the face of the massed Confederate attack, Lee changed his mind. The Federal retreat looked just like those in the previous campaigns that had ended in Confederate victories.

Still, Lee had to act fast if he wanted to end the battle decisively. The Federals were working hard at fortifying Cemetery Hill. The Southern commander knew that if he did not sweep the Union soldiers off this hill soon, they would be strong enough to withstand attack until reinforcements arrived.

The very ill A. P. Hill, who had managed with great effort finally to reach Gettysburg, agreed with Lee. However, he could not send his troops to attack Cemetery Hill. The two divisions of Third Corps that were present were too shot up and too worn out to fight any more that day.

The view of Gettysburg from Cemetery Hill. Along this road the Federals retreated toward Cemetery Hill on the afternoon of July 1. The road on the left is the Baltimore pike.

Lee then sent word to Ewell asking Second Corps to attack the Federal position. Lee believed that Ewell's men were in better shape than Hill's, particularly those in Early's division that had taken very few casualties in the fighting.

However, after discussing Lee's request with his division commanders, Rodes and Early, Ewell decided it would be foolhardy to attack. The Federal position was too strong, and Cemetery Hill was too difficult to scale in the face of firm resistance, particularly with soldiers tired from the afternoon's hard fighting.

Hancock Arrives on Cemetery Hill

Meanwhile, Hancock arrived on the top of Cemetery Hill at about 4:15 P.M. Looking around he saw as one of his staff later reported, "wreck, disaster, disorder, . . . defeat and retreat were everywhere."

Yet, the battle was far from lost. True, the Federals had been driven from their original position, but their new one was actually superior. A quarter mile east of Cemetery Hill and connected to it by a high, steep land bridge was the slightly taller Culp's Hill. The two mounds formed a natural fortress.

South of Cemetery and Culp's Hills ran the broad Cemetery Ridge, which ended after about two miles in two more hills, Little Round Top and Round Top. Little Round Top was 170 feet high and Round Top, 300 feet. The heights formed a letter *J* whose head was the Round Tops; shank, Cemetery Ridge; and hook, Cemetery and Culp's Hills.

Hancock told Howard, "Very well, sir, I select this as the battlefield." He sent this message back to Meade and began organizing his defenses.

Little Round Top would be the site of vicious fighting on the second day of the Battle of Gettysburg. The hillside after the battle was literally strewn with the dead and wounded.

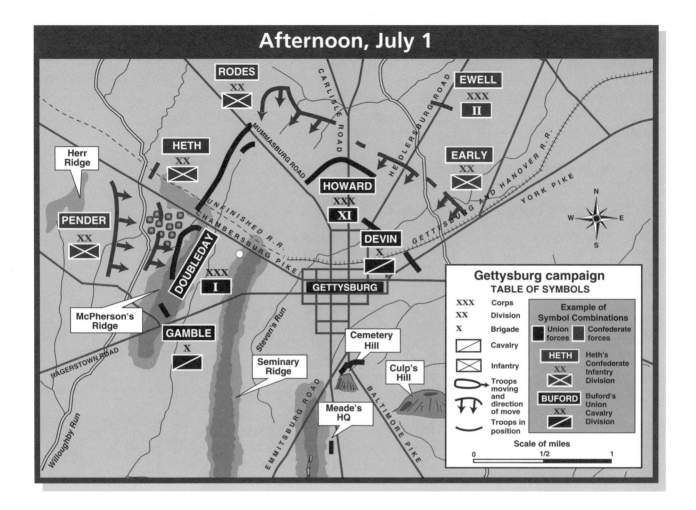

Afternoon, July 1

One of Hancock's first acts was to order Doubleday to put troops on Culp's Hill. If the Confederates gained the top of this higher neighbor of Cemetery Hill, their firepower could easily force the Union soldiers to withdraw.

Hancock had arrived without any support except his personal staff, but his air of confidence and competence was enough to boost the morale of the weary Federal troops. General Carl Schurz said later that "his [Hancock's] mere presence was a reinforcement, and everybody on the field felt stronger for his being there."

Soon, however, the Federals on Cemetery Hill received actual reinforcements when Slocum's Twelfth Corps arrived at 6:00 P.M. Not far behind was Third Corps. The Army of the Potomac was gathering.

Longstreet Advises Lee

While Hancock worked out the Federal defense on Cemetery and Culp's Hills, Lee waited for Ewell to attack. He would not know until later that Ewell had decided not to assault the Federal high ground.

Lee sat on his horse, Traveller, and surveyed Gettysburg through his binoculars. As he was doing so, Longstreet rode up and joined him. Old Pete had ridden ahead of his own marching troops to look over the battlefield for himself.

The First Corps commander immediately pointed out to Lee that the Confederates could take control of the still deserted Round Tops. From these hills, higher than both Cemetery and Culp's Hills, they could bombard the Union soldiers with artillery and either force them to retreat or attack uphill against the Southern army.

Lee, however, had set his sights on Cemetery Hill. Pointing in the direction of the Union trenches, Lee said, "The enemy is there, and I am going to attack him there." Longstreet replied, "If the enemy is there, it is because he is anxious that we should attack him: a good reason . . . for not doing so."

Lee refused to change his mind, and in doing so, made a serious mistake, one that would eventually cost him the battle. He would come to agree with Longstreet about the Round Tops, but by then, it would be too late. The hills would be in Federal hands.

Why did Lee dismiss Longstreet's sound advice? As Old Pete later wrote, "When the hunt was up, his [Lee's] combativeness was overruling." The Southern commander wanted to attack the Federals, and that desire left little room for reason. Also, as historian James McPherson observes:

> He [Lee] had not accomplished the hoped-for "destruction" of the enemy in . . . [previous campaigns]. Gettysburg presented him with . . . [another] chance. The morale of his veteran troops had never been higher; they would regard such a maneuver as Longstreet suggested as a retreat . . . and lose their fighting edge.

Day One's Final Count

Around 7:30 P.M., Lee rode over to Ewell's unit to discover what had happened to the proposed attack against Cemetery Hill. When the Southern commander found out that the Second Corps was not going to scramble up the hill, the day's fighting was finally over. Of that fighting, one Confederate officer said, "I have taken part in many hotly contested fights, but this I think was the deadliest of them all."

And deadly Gettysburg's first day of combat had been: 12,000 Union troops and 8,000 Confederates were killed or wounded. The Federal army's Twenty-fourth Michigan Regiment, part of the Iron Brigade, for example, lost all but 97 of its 496 officers and men. Two Confederate companies of the Twenty-sixth North Carolina Regiment suffered even heavier losses. Only 2 of their 174 soldiers staggered out of the battle unhurt.

Behind the stark numbers was the reality of death and the pain of injury. Men had died after being riddled by rifle balls, blown apart by artillery shells, and stabbed with bayonets.

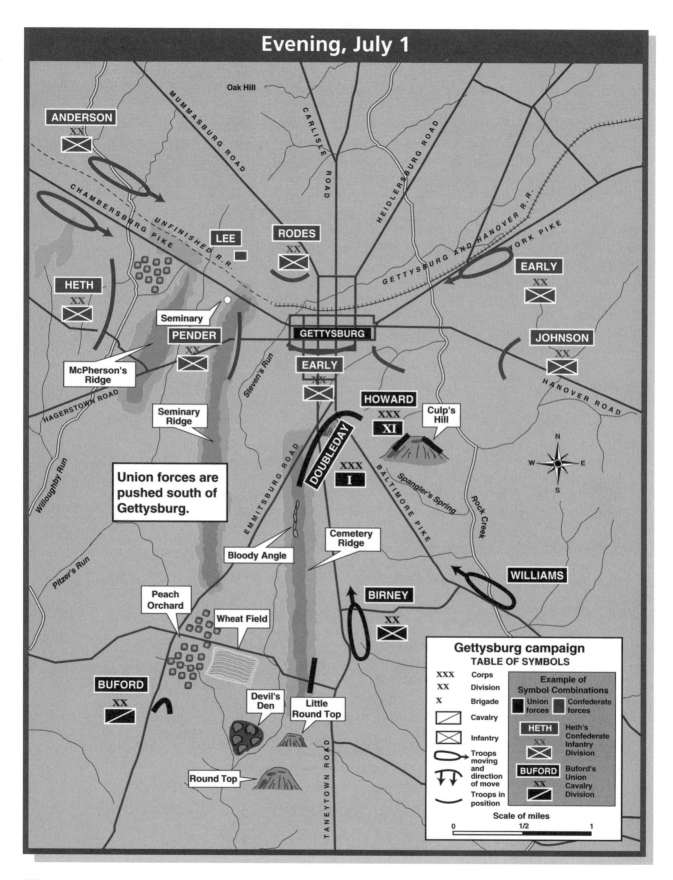

Evening, July 1

ANDERSON

Oak Hill

MUMMASBURG ROAD

CARLISLE ROAD

HEIDLERSBURG ROAD

GETTYSBURG AND HANOVER R.R.

YORK PIKE

CHAMBERSBURG PIKE

UNFINISHED R.R.

LEE

RODES

EARLY

GETTYSBURG AND HANOVER

HETH

Seminary

PENDER

McPherson's Ridge

HAGERSTOWN ROAD

Seminary Ridge

GETTYSBURG

JOHNSON

HANOVER ROAD

Steven's Run

EARLY

HOWARD

XI

Culp's Hill

DOUBLEDAY

Spangler's Spring

BALTIMORE PIKE

Rock Creek

Union forces are pushed south of Gettysburg.

Willoughby Run

EMMITSBURG ROAD

I

Cemetery Ridge

WILLIAMS

Pitzer's Run

Bloody Angle

Peach Orchard

Wheat Field

BIRNEY

BUFORD

Devil's Den

Little Round Top

Round Top

TANEYTOWN ROAD

Gettysburg campaign
TABLE OF SYMBOLS

XXX	Corps
XX	Division
X	Brigade

Example of Symbol Combinations

Union forces — Confederate forces

HETH — Heth's Confederate Infantry Division

BUFORD — Buford's Union Cavalry Division

Cavalry

Infantry

Troops moving and direction of move

Troops in position

Scale of miles

0   1/2   1

Members of the Twenty-fourth Michigan Regiment lie dead after the first day at Gettysburg. Before nightfall, Confederates would strip these men of shoes, ammunition, and weapons— anything the desperately underequipped army could use.

The wounded, many of whom would die in agony during the night, lay everywhere. Their screams were "dreadful howls," according to one Southern soldier. They bled from bullet holes, from stumps from which arms and legs had been blown off, and from sliced-open bodies.

Despite the blood and gore, neither side retreated. As night fell, the two armies prepared for day two of the Battle of Gettysburg.

CHAPTER FOUR

Day Two: We Will Sell Out as Dearly as Possible

The second day of the Battle of Gettysburg, Thursday, July 2, 1863, was even hotter and muggier than the day before. Fog in the morning and drizzling rain in the afternoon did little to cool things off.

Sweat soaked the uniforms of the men of both the Army of the Potomac and the Army of Northern Virginia as they fought a series of fierce actions. Hard fighting in the smothering heat eventually drained the strength from even the strongest soldier, and all were exhausted.

Still, the armies fought. The Federals ended the day in control of all the high ground from Cemetery Hill to Little Round Top. The day's combat gave the Confederates a shaky foothold on the edge of Culp's Hill but little else.

The Army of the Potomac owed its success in part to the capable leadership of a number of its officers. But in larger part, that success was because of the steadfastness and bravery of its soldiers, who paid a terrible bloody price to throw back the supposedly unbeatable Army of Northern Virginia. As one Pennsylvania sergeant said, "We've got to fight our best today or have these rebs [Confederates] for our masters!"

Meade Arrives at Gettysburg

Just before dawn on July 2, Army of the Potomac commander George Meade finally arrived at Gettysburg. Upon receiving Hancock's messages about the battleground the previous evening, Meade had decided to order all his remaining troops to the Penn-

(Right) The headquarters on Cemetery Ridge that Meade occupied on July 2 and 3. Meade and his staff would be driven from this building on July 3. (Above) Union soldiers face off against the Confederates on Little Round Top.

sylvania town. By the time Meade arrived, only the Army of the Potomac's Fifth and Sixth Corps were still on the march to Gettysburg.

Meade set up his headquarters on the eastern side of Cemetery Ridge in the cemetery caretaker's house. He called together his corps commanders and reviewed the details of the Federal defense. He inspected the battle site at first light and indicated where he wanted to station specific units.

The Union commander liked what he saw, fully agreeing with Hancock that Gettysburg was the place for a major battle. There was, of course, the natural fortress of the two northern hills. But in addition, Cemetery Ridge, which averaged twenty to thirty feet in height, gave his soldiers an excellent platform from which to fight, even though it did drop off to ground level just before Little Round Top. The ridge's western slope, the one facing the

Confederates, was steep and covered with a jumble of rocks and a tangle of plants.

The flat ground in front of Cemetery Ridge would not provide the Confederates with much protective cover. Only an occasional building, orchard, or clump of trees broke the generally open farmland.

Meade Organizes His Defenses

Meade spread his troops from the eastern and northern faces of Culp's Hill to the foot of Little Round Top. Slocum's Twelfth Corps and one division of First Corps occupied Culp's Hill and the land bridge that connected it to Cemetery Hill. Howard's Eleventh Corps remained atop the latter hill.

Hancock's Second Corps held the first stretch of Cemetery Ridge, which was also the center of the Union line. The remainder of First Corps, now under the command of General John Newton, provided backup protection. Sickles's Third Corps took the southern length of the ridge, the Union army's southern flank. Sykes's newly arrived Fifth Corps was left on the eastern side of Cemetery Ridge to provide support for the frontline troops.

Several units of artillery were placed where Cemetery Ridge and Cemetery Hill joined, at a height of eighty feet. From this position the big guns could send shells over the entire battlefront. Reserve artillery was stationed on the eastern side of Cemetery Ridge near Fifth Corps.

Lee Plans His Strategy

As Meade readied his defenses, Lee also prepared for the day's fighting. The Southern commander had gotten up an hour before dawn and began reviewing his plans. His headquarters tent was nestled on the western side of Seminary Ridge, about a mile west of Cemetery Ridge. Seminary Ridge rose to a height of almost two hundred feet and took its name from the Lutheran seminary, or training school for ministers, on its crest.

Lee had decided to send Longstreet's First Corps against the Federal southern flank. Old Pete would hit the Union line at the point where Cemetery Ridge sank low.

To help Longstreet's assault, Ewell's Second Corps was to launch an attack against Cemetery and Culp's Hills. The northern strike would be a diversion, unless the Second Corps commander believed that he could actually capture the hills. Ewell's signal to attack was to be the sound of Longstreet's artillery opening fire. Hill's Third Corps was to provide a reserve of troops to back up the First and Second Corps.

Longstreet's assault was expected to begin in the early morning. However, his corps did not start reaching Gettysburg until

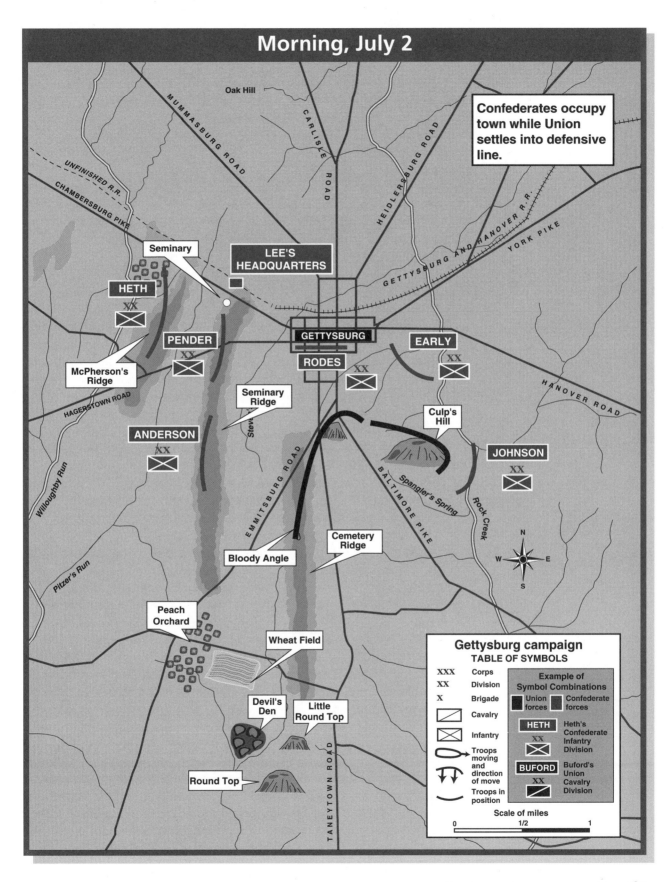

Morning, July 2

Confederates occupy town while Union settles into defensive line.

Oak Hill

MUMMASBURG ROAD

CARLISLE ROAD

HEIDLERSBURG ROAD

UNFINISHED R.R.

CHAMBERSBURG PIKE

GETTYSBURG AND HANOVER R.R.

YORK PIKE

Seminary

LEE'S HEADQUARTERS

HETH
XX

PENDER
XX

McPherson's Ridge

GETTYSBURG

RODES
XX

EARLY
XX

HANOVER ROAD

HAGERSTOWN ROAD

Seminary Ridge

Steve

Culp's Hill

JOHNSON
XX

ANDERSON
XX

Willoughby Run

EMMITSBURG ROAD

Spangler's Spring

BALTIMORE PIKE

Rock Creek

N
W   E
S

Bloody Angle

Cemetery Ridge

Pitzer's Run

Peach Orchard

Wheat Field

Devil's Den

Little Round Top

TANEYTOWN ROAD

Round Top

Gettysburg campaign
TABLE OF SYMBOLS

XXX	Corps
XX	Division
X	Brigade

Example of Symbol Combinations

Union forces (black) / Confederate forces (gray)

| HETH | Heth's Confederate Infantry Division |
| XX | |

| BUFORD | Buford's Union Cavalry Division |
| XX | |

Cavalry

Infantry

Troops moving and direction of move

Troops in position

Scale of miles

0   1/2   1

after 8:00 A.M. By midmorning, two First Corps divisions, led by Generals John B. Hood and Lafayette McLaws, were on hand. First Corps's third division, commanded by General George E. Pickett, would not reach Gettysburg in time to take part in the second day's fighting. One of Hood's brigades was also missing, but except for these units and Stuart's cavalry, the entire Army of Northern Virginia was now gathered together at Gettysburg.

Longstreet Objects to Lee's Plan

Longstreet once more objected to Lee's plans. To the First Corps leader, Lee's proposed assault was a suicidal gamble. Old Pete thought that attacking the Union troops would produce high casualties and hold a very slight chance of victory.

Longstreet suggested instead that the Army of Northern Virginia swing south. Such a move would put the Confederates between the Army of the Potomac and Washington, D.C., forcing Meade to come off the heights to attack the Southern army on ground of the latter's choosing. If Lee did not want to shift south, then Longstreet believed that the Army of Northern Virginia should stay put and not attack the better-placed Northern army.

Lee pointed out that moving south was risky. Without the cavalry to spy out the enemy's movements, the Confederates had no idea where the bulk of the Army of the Potomac was. The Southern army could well swing south right into the path of most of Meade's troops.

As for sitting on and behind Seminary Ridge, that too was dangerous. Within a few days the Army of Northern Virginia could find itself pinned between the Army of the Potomac and Union reinforcements coming from the west.

Lee believed that he had no choice but to order Longstreet and Ewell to attack the Federal line. Besides, he thought the chances of success much better than did Longstreet. Lee still believed that the soldiers of the Army of Northern Virginia were the best in the world and certainly better than any Federal troops. Union soldier Warren Gross later said that the confidence of Lee's soldiers "to defeat the Yankees [the Federals] at all times and under all circumstances [was] so great that Lee himself, with all his equipoise [balance] of character, caught something of this overconfidence."

Longstreet's First Corps Takes Its Position

Longstreet had no choice, of course, but to obey Lee, although he delayed moving his troops until Hood's missing brigade arrived. At noon McLaws's and Hood's divisions began moving south. They marched along the far side of Herr Ridge, about two miles west of the Federal line, so as to hide their movements from the Federals.

The Springfield Rifle

Both Confederate and Federal infantry units used many different types of rifles during the Civil War. The most common one was the Springfield, named for Springfield, Massachusetts, where most of the guns were made.

The Union army made or bought about 1.5 million Springfields during the Civil War. The South had fewer, many of them taken from Federal arsenals that fell into Confederate hands or from stocks captured during battles and raids. Other Southern Springfields were made at the Confederate Armory in Richmond, Virginia.

The Springfield weighed nine pounds and was nearly five feet long. It fired a single shot and was accurate up to a quarter mile. At close range—anything under a thousand feet—it was deadly, as seen in this description by Confederate general John Gordon: "My [unit's] rifles flamed and roared in the Federals' faces. . . . The effect was appalling. The entire front line . . . went down in the . . . blast."

To load the Springfield, a soldier took a paper-wrapped package holding gunpowder and a bullet from his belt pouch. He bit off the cartridge's end, poured the powder down the barrel, and pushed the bullet in with a ramrod. Experienced soldiers could load and fire three times a minute.

Nervous or exhausted soldiers sometimes loaded their rifles wrong and put the guns out of action. They might carelessly insert the bullet before the powder or jam several cartridges down the barrel. (One rifle found on the Gettysburg battlefield had been loaded with twenty-three cartridges!) Others simply forgot to remove the ramrod before shooting.

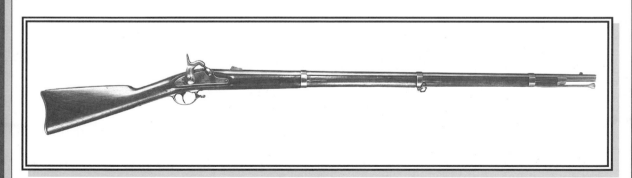

The Springfield musket rifle was a standard weapon during the Civil War.

Marching into Battle

What was it like to fight in the Civil War? Even in good weather, it was hot, sweaty work, often done with little water, food, or sleep.

To get into position, the soldiers endure a grueling march that lasts for hours. Thus, even before combat begins, they are tired. After an hour or two of fighting, these weary soldiers will be close to physical collapse.

Now, finally approaching the battle, the troops hear the distant boom of artillery. They pass the field hospital where they see stacks of cut-off arms and legs and rows of uncovered bodies. The soldiers make grim jokes to hide their unease at these sights.

The marching men see smoke everywhere. Civil War gunpowder is not smokeless like later powders will be. The soldiers can see only the battle flags waving above the gun smoke.

The noise of battle deafens them. Cannons roar, rifles and revolvers crackle, drums beat, and trumpets sound. Officers and sergeants shout orders, soldiers curse and cheer, and the wounded shriek and scream in pain.

A few of the soldiers refuse to go any farther. Most, however, unsling their rifles and advance.

Hours later many lie dead or wounded. The survivors look around, numb and dazed by the noise and confusion of combat. Their hands and faces are smeared with black gunpowder. Those who are unhurt can now look forward to some rest until the next round of fighting.

Longstreet and his division commanders did not conduct the march well. Several confused units went to the wrong place. These wayward troops then had to keep on hiking until they reached their correct positions. The extra marching and counter-marching meant that First Corps was not ready to attack until late afternoon.

The First Corps's march was grueling. Some of McLaws's and Hood's soldiers hiked more than twelve miles in the blistering afternoon heat. The heat and humidity sucked the water out of the men's bodies, and they had little water with them. The soldiers of Hood's late-arriving brigade were also fatigued from lack of sleep because they had spent most of the previous night on a forced march to Gettysburg.

Face to Face

When Lee's troops were finally in place, the Army of Northern Virginia's line made an arc running west from Culp's Hill, south along Seminary Ridge, and then back east to Round Top. Richard Ewell's Second Corps formed the left flank, facing Cemetery and Culp's Hills.

Two divisions of A. P. Hill's Third Corps stretched along the middle of Seminary Ridge, almost directly across from the center of the Union line on Cemetery Ridge. The remaining Third Corps division, Heth's badly battered unit, sat in reserve on the west side of the ridge. Longstreet's First Corps faced northeast toward the end of Cemetery Ridge. Its right flank almost touched Round Top.

The arc that Lee's army formed was almost six miles long. It challenged a Federal line that was less than a mile long. The spread of the Southern army would make it hard for their reinforcements to reach trouble spots quickly. The clustering of the Union army would make the movement of such reinforcements much faster and easier.

Longstreet Attacks

Longstreet was still uneasy about the proposed assault, and his mood was evident. As one soldier observed, Longstreet, with "his eyes cast to the ground, as if in deep study, his mind disturbed [had] the look of gloom." However, he was determined to carry out Lee's orders no matter what.

At 4:00 P.M., Longstreet told Hood to take his men in. McLaws was to follow one hour later. Both divisions were to sweep across the flat farmland and hit the southern flank of the Federal line on Cemetery Ridge.

The only problem with this plan was that the Federal flank was not on the ridge. Much to Hood's surprise, Confederate scouts spotted it a half mile west of the rise.

Longstreet consults with his staff on July 2 at Gettysburg. The Confederates would lose many men as a result of Longstreet's following of Lee's flawed orders.

Hood urged Longstreet to change the battle plan so that the Southern troops would not ride into heavy Federal fire. The division leader suggested going farther south and attacking from around the Round Tops.

Longstreet rejected Hood's suggestion. He told Hood that Lee had ordered an attack on the southern end of Cemetery Ridge, not on the Round Tops. "We must obey the orders of General Lee," Longstreet said.

Old Pete did not even bother telling Lee about the Union flank's new position. He had tried twice to change his commander's mind. He would not try a third time. Instead, he ordered Hood to attack immediately.

Sickles and Third Corps Move Forward

The Federal unit west of Cemetery Ridge was indeed Sickles's Third Corps, whom Meade had assigned to be on the Union army's southern flank. Sickles's men were occupying a peach orchard

General Daniel Sickles's decision to ignore orders and reposition his troops off Cemetery Ridge left Hancock's troops exposed.

directly west of their original position on the ridge, as well as a maze of boulders and stunted trees at the base of Little Round Top called the Devil's Den.

If Hood was surprised at finding Union soldiers in front of Cemetery Ridge, Army of the Potomac commander Meade was even more so. Sickles was out there without orders. The Northern commander discovered Sickles's move when he rode up to check on the Confederate attack beginning in the south.

Sickles thought his troops were too exposed on the southern end of the ridge, which turned into low, marshy ground before rising into Little Round Top. Without telling Meade his intention, the Third Corps leader moved his men off the ridge to ground that looked safer. Sickles did not even tell Hancock, whose Second Corps was now exposed to attack from the south around the Round Tops, the very strategy that Hood had urged and that Longstreet had rejected.

Upon discovering Sickles's position, Meade immediately called for Sykes's Fifth Corps to take the abandoned place of Third Corps. Sickles offered to bring his troops back to Cemetery Ridge. Meade, however, pointed to the approaching Confederates and said, "It is too late. The enemy will not allow you."

Struggle for the Peach Orchard

Whether or not Sickles was right to move forward, his troops fought hard against the surging Confederate attack. The Third Corps was outnumbered, but the Union soldiers did not break and run under the Confederate pressure. They continued to fight, slowing the rush of Hood's division toward the Union line.

The fighting in the Peach Orchard was some of the heaviest of the battle. As Union colonel P. Regis de Trobriand later observed:

It was a hard fight. The Confederates appeared to have the devil in them. My men did not flinch and, then when their assailants . . . [attacked], they were received with a deadly volley, every shot of which was effective. . . . On both sides, each one [each soldier] aimed at his man, and men fell dead and wounded with frightful rapidity.

The combat even cost both sides division commanders. A cannonball took off one of Sickles's legs, and an artillery shell fragment shattered one of Hood's arms.

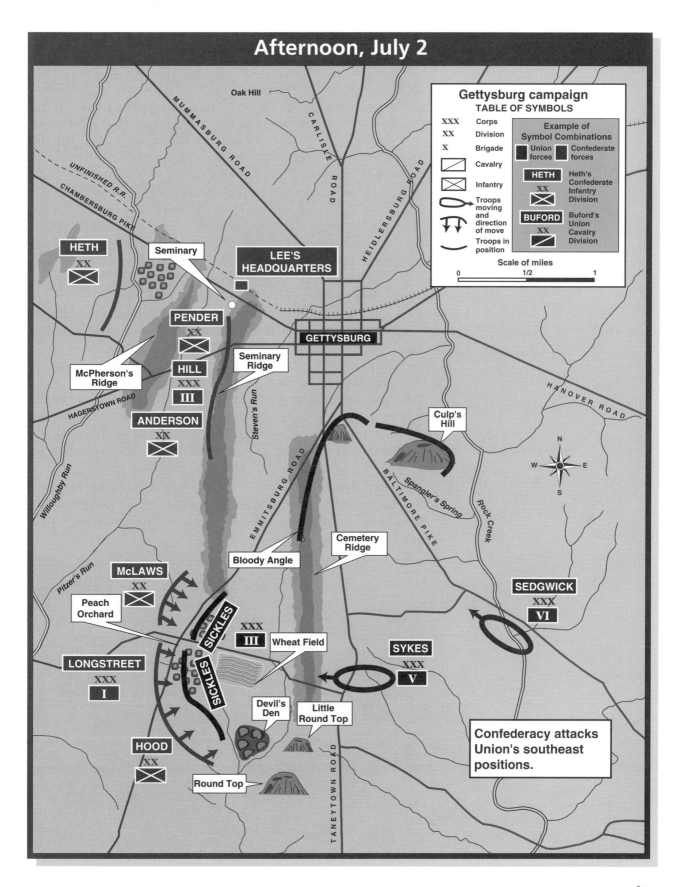

Afternoon, July 2

Oak Hill

MUMMASBURG ROAD

CARLISLE ROAD

UNFINISHED R.R.

CHAMBERSBURG PIKE

HEIDLERSBURG ROAD

Gettysburg campaign
TABLE OF SYMBOLS

XXX	Corps
XX	Division
X	Brigade

Cavalry

Infantry

Troops moving and direction of move

Troops in position

Example of Symbol Combinations

| Union forces | Confederate forces |

HETH Heth's Confederate Infantry Division
XX

BUFORD Buford's Union Cavalry Division
XX

Scale of miles
0   1/2   1

HETH
XX

Seminary

LEE'S HEADQUARTERS

PENDER
XX

Seminary Ridge

McPherson's Ridge

HILL
XXX
III

HAGERSTOWN ROAD

ANDERSON
XX

Steven's Run

GETTYSBURG

HANOVER ROAD

Culp's Hill

Spangler's Spring

BALTIMORE PIKE

Rock Creek

Willoughby Run

EMMITSBURG ROAD

Bloody Angle

Cemetery Ridge

N
W   E
S

Pitzer's Run

McLAWS
XX

Peach Orchard

SICKLES
XXX
III

Wheat Field

SICKLES

SEDGWICK
XXX
VI

SYKES
XXX
V

LONGSTREET
XXX
I

Devil's Den

Little Round Top

TANEYTOWN ROAD

Confederacy attacks Union's southeast positions.

HOOD
XX

Round Top

Defending Little Round Top

The fighting in the Devil's Den was just as bad as that in the Peach Orchard. Since this rocky jumble lay at the foot of Little Round Top, many of Hood's soldiers abandoned the ground combat to climb to the hill's summit. The Confederates believed that no Federal troops occupied Little Round Top and that the hill would be an easy route to the Union line on Cemetery Ridge, as well as being a prize position.

The Confederates were correct about Little Round Top's not having Union defenders on it. However, as Hood's men prepared to climb the hill, one of Meade's staff officers, General Gouverneur K. Warren, who had climbed the hill to look at the fighting below, spotted them. Realizing that it was crucial to keep Little Round Top, which overlooked the entire Federal line, out of Lee's hands, Warren rushed to Fifth Corps to find help.

Fifth Corps commander Sykes was willing to send a brigade and told Warren to have division leader General James Barnes provide one. Warren could not find Barnes but located Colonel Strong Vincent, who also recognized how catastrophic the loss of Little Round Top would be.

Without permission and ignoring his current orders, the colonel took his brigade on the run to Little Round Top. Reaching the top of the hill, Vincent placed the four regiments of his brigade at critical spots along the southern and western edges of the summit.

If Vincent had hesitated or been slower, he and his men would have found Little Round Top occupied by Confederates. Fifteen minutes after they arrived, Southern soldiers stormed up the hill's western slope.

A Confederate sharpshooter lies dead in the Devil's Den. The position became a stronghold for the sharpshooters, who continued to pick off Union soldiers and officers even when being heavily shelled by Union batteries.

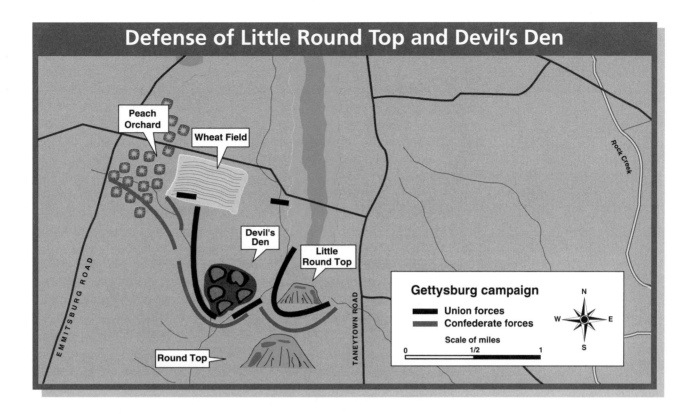

Defense of Little Round Top and Devil's Den

Labels on map: Peach Orchard, Wheat Field, Devil's Den, Little Round Top, Round Top, Rock Creek, EMMITSBURG ROAD, TANEYTOWN ROAD

Gettysburg campaign
— Union forces
— Confederate forces
Scale of miles
0   1/2   1

N
W   E
S

The Twentieth Maine Holds Its Position

Vincent gave the defense of the southeastern edge to Colonel Joshua L. Chamberlain, who had been a professor of modern languages before the war. "Hold at all hazard" was Chamberlain's instruction, and that was exactly what the 385 men of the Twentieth Maine Regiment did.

Chamberlain's regiment was soon exchanging heavy fire with the five hundred soldiers of Colonel William C. Oates's Fifteenth Alabama Regiment. Oates would later say, "Within half an hour I could convert Little Round Top into a . . . [fortress] that I could hold against ten times the number of men I had." Oates never got that half hour.

Chamberlain and his troops drove Oates and his men off Little Round Top. It took an hour of hard fighting, during which the Federals used up twenty thousand rounds of ammunition. The Twentieth Maine was so low on bullets that it had to finish the action against the Fifteenth Alabama with a bayonet charge.

In the end, both units paid a high price for winning and losing their battle on Little Round Top. The Twentieth Maine lost a third of its men, while the Fifteenth Alabama lost almost half. As one soldier of the Twentieth Maine later observed, "Not only on the crest of the hill among the bluecoats was blood running in little rivulets [small streams] and forming crimson pools, but in the gray ranks . . . there had also been fearful destruction."

The Battle for Little Round Top's Western Summit

Things were not going so well for the Federal defenders on the western side of Little Round Top. Vincent's remaining regiments were crumpling under the combined attack of two Confederate brigades. Vincent was mortally wounded while trying to rally his troops, and the Confederates were close to sweeping his regiment off the hill.

Once more, it was General Gouverneur Warren who saved the hill for the Federals. Warren would later be called "The Savior of Little Round Top."

(Right and below) Dead soldiers are mute testimony to the crescendo of carnage that marked the struggle for Little Round Top. (Below, right) General Gouverneur Warren's quick thinking saved the crucial hill from falling to the Confederates when he noticed it was undefended and posted Vincent's troops in the nick of time.

The general was helping to set up some artillery for the Federal defense of the hill when he learned that the western defense of Little Round Top was falling apart. Spying a brigade marching toward the Peach Orchard, Warren rode down and stopped it.

This unit also belonged to Fifth Corps and originally had been on its way to Little Round Top. However, the unit had run into Sickles, who ordered it to the Peach Orchard to help his Third Corps. The brigade continued on to the Peach Orchard but not before Warren pried loose a regiment of 450 soldiers.

The regimental leader, Colonel Patrick H. O'Rorke, ran his men to the top of Little Round Top. There, with rifles empty and not having had time to load, the reinforcements fixed bayonets and threw themselves into the fight. Many Fifth Corps soldiers were killed, including O'Rorke, but the regiment slowed the Confederate sweep of Little Round Top.

Minutes later, the remainder of the regiment's brigade appeared. Sykes, discovering that Sickles had seized the unit, had caught up with it and ordered its commander once more to Little Round Top.

The additional fifteen hundred Union troops turned the tide and thrust the Confederates off and down Little Round Top. Sykes kept sending troops until a full division occupied the contested height, which was now firmly in Federal hands.

Confused Fighting in the Federal Center

Little Round Top was secure but the same could not be said for the center of the Union line. Sickles's Third Corps was taking a pounding, and his troops' ability to hold their position was becoming increasingly difficult.

Sickles stripped brigades from one Third Corps division to reinforce the other. His division commanders, in turn, swapped regiments between brigades to counter Confederate assaults. Bluecoated soldiers ran from one part of the central battlefield to another, often completely confused about where they were going and what they were doing.

Sickles had even gotten Meade's permission to pull in units from other corps to help in the fighting. According to historian Albert Nofi:

> This practice did little for the morale or the cohesion [unity] of the affected troops. Forced to participate in . . . actions under unknown officers with strange units on their flanks . . . , the men could not perform to the best of their abilities.

The confusion became worse when Sickles was wounded and left the field. No one immediately stepped forward to direct the defense, but the arrival of four additional brigades, two from

Civil War Rations

Civil War soldiers on both sides ate similar kinds of food, although the Confederate army generally issued smaller portions and often ran short of rations. In camp the troops had bread, salt pork, beans, dried potatoes, dried vegetables, coffee, sugar, salt, and vinegar.

The salt pork had to be soaked for hours to get rid of the brine before it could be cooked. It was then often just stuck on a bayonet or sharp stick and held over a fire. The vegetables came in a small, pressed block that was cooked in boiling water.

On the march, rations were much reduced, consisting only of salt pork, coffee, sugar, salt, and a large, thick cracker called hardtack. Hardtack was often moldy and filled with weevils or maggots, and the soldiers would crumble it into a cup of boiling coffee and skim the weevils off as they floated to the surface.

The Union soldiers loved coffee. Each soldier carried a bag of coffee beans, crushing up the beans with his rifle butt. Any stop was an occasion for soldiers to build fires and brew coffee.

The Union even experimented with instant coffee, which was a mixture of coffee, milk, and sugar. One teaspoon of this coffee essence, as it was called, made a cup of coffee. However, the soldiers did not like it, and the army stopped issuing it.

Second Corps and two from Fifth Corps, helped steady the Union line. The reinforcements fought the Confederates to a standstill. Two more Fifth Corps brigades rushed up, and suddenly they were overpowering the Southern soldiers.

Longstreet Leads the Charge

Hood's sixty-eight hundred soldiers faced ten thousand Federals. The Southern troops needed help, and it came from McLaws's division, which now joined the battle.

The fighting seesawed back and forth. First, Confederate troops would gain an edge, then Union, and so on. During this long afternoon of fighting, the Wheat Field in front of the Peach Orchard changed hands four times before the Southern army finally claimed it.

Normally, a corps commander was expected to stay in the rear and direct his unit's efforts. However, Longstreet became so concerned about the difficulty his troops were having that he led one of McLaws's brigades into the thick of the fight. As he rushed by, his men cheered. Longstreet called out, "Cheer less, men, and fight more!"

The Union's Center Holds

In the end, nothing Longstreet did made any difference. The Army of Northern Virginia's First Corps did not break the Army of the Potomac's center. By late afternoon, the Army of the Potomac's Sixth Corps began arriving and added its soldiers to the battle. The Federal troops then took up positions once more on Cemetery Ridge.

However, the fighting in the center was not over. A gap remained where Sickles's Third Corps was supposed to have been, and Confederate general Richard H. Anderson's division, part of Hill's Third Corps, came close to thrusting through that hole in the Union line.

Around 6:00 P.M., Anderson's troops charged down Seminary Ridge and across the valley to smash into the Federal line on Cemetery Ridge. One Alabama brigade, commanded by General Cadmus M. Wilcox, headed straight for the Union army's weak spot. "On they came like the fury of a whirlwind," said one Union officer.

Hancock, who was now in charge of both Second and Third Corps, saw Wilcox and his soldiers coming. He immediately called for reinforcements but knew that they would be at least five minutes in coming. By then, the Alabamians would be through the Union line.

Looking around for some way to slow down the Confederate charge, Hancock spotted the First Minnesota regiment coming over the crest of the ridge. The corps commander stopped the unit and, pointing to the Alabama brigade's battle flag, asked the regiment's colonel, "Colonel, do you see those colors?" Hancock followed this question with "Then take them."

It was an impossible request, but the 262 Minnesotans fixed their bayonets, ran forward, and attacked the seventeen hundred Alabamians. Taken by surprise, the Confederates fell back. Wilcox's recovering men blasted away at the First Minnesota, killing or wounding all but forty-seven of the Federal regiment's members.

The First Minnesota paid a heavy price for its action, but it also gave Hancock ten life-saving minutes to regroup. By then, the Union reinforcements were in the Federal line, and their combined firepower forced Wilcox's brigade to retreat.

Continued fierce resistance on the part of the Union soldiers finally stopped the Confederate attack. The gap in the Northern army's line was finally filled with units from Slocum's Twelfth Corps. Once more, the Federal soldiers held their ground.

Ewell Launches His Attack

But, even as the battle for the Union center came to an end, new fighting erupted in the north. This time Ewell's Second Corps was attacking Cemetery Hill and Culp's Hill.

Around 6:00 P.M., Ewell issued orders for all three of his divisions to attack the two northern hills. However, he did a poor job of overseeing the operation, and consequently, Rodes's division never even got itself going and missed the combat entirely. Later, Ewell would admit that he had handled his command badly. The Second Corps commander confided to a friend, "It took a dozen blunders to lose Gettysburg and [I] committed a good many of them."

The Fight for Cemetery and Culp's Hills

Early's Second Corps division, composed of veterans, did well at first. They streamed across the ground to the foot of Cemetery Hill and then quickly scrambled up its slope. Howard's Eleventh Corps, which had been badly chewed up in the previous day's fighting, was at the top to meet them.

That night the Federals and the Confederates engaged in hand-to-hand combat among the tombstones. General Carl Schurz, an Eleventh Corps division commander, sent two regiments into the fray with bayonets and then followed along with his staff.

In the end, reinforcements from Second Corps helped the struggling Eleventh Corps troops push Early's men back off Cemetery Hill. The Union soldiers followed the retreating Con-

Southern general Jubal Early (right) made a valiant attempt to take Cemetery Hill, but a final push by Union forces (above) secured the hill before the end of the second day.

federates down the slope, clearing them from the foot of the hill. By 10:30 P.M., Early's threat to Cemetery Hill was over.

Ewell's third division commander, General Edward Johnson, had more success than Early. He and his men stormed Culp's Hill and managed to gain a foothold on its northeastern edge. The Union defenders were Slocum's Twelfth Corps, part of which had gone to reinforce the Federal center. However, with the fighting on Cemetery Ridge ended, other Twelfth Corps units began to return, and their rifles helped stop Johnson from taking more of the hill.

Day Two Finally Ends

Thus, the second day of the Battle of Gettysburg ended. Historian Bruce Catton writes:

> This . . . day . . . [had been] made up of many separate fights, each one a moment or an hour of concentrated fury, with a blinding, choking fog of blue powder smoke over the hillsides and the rocky woods, hammered down by unending deafening noise, sparkling and glowing evilly with constant spurts of fire.

The Army of the Potomac had lost nine thousand men, but they had secured their line from Cemetery Hill to Little Round Top. The smaller Army of Northern Virginia had taken the same number of casualties as the Union army. However, they had failed to capture either Cemetery Hill or Little Round Top, and they had not broken the Union line. Their only victory was a small bit of Culp's Hill.

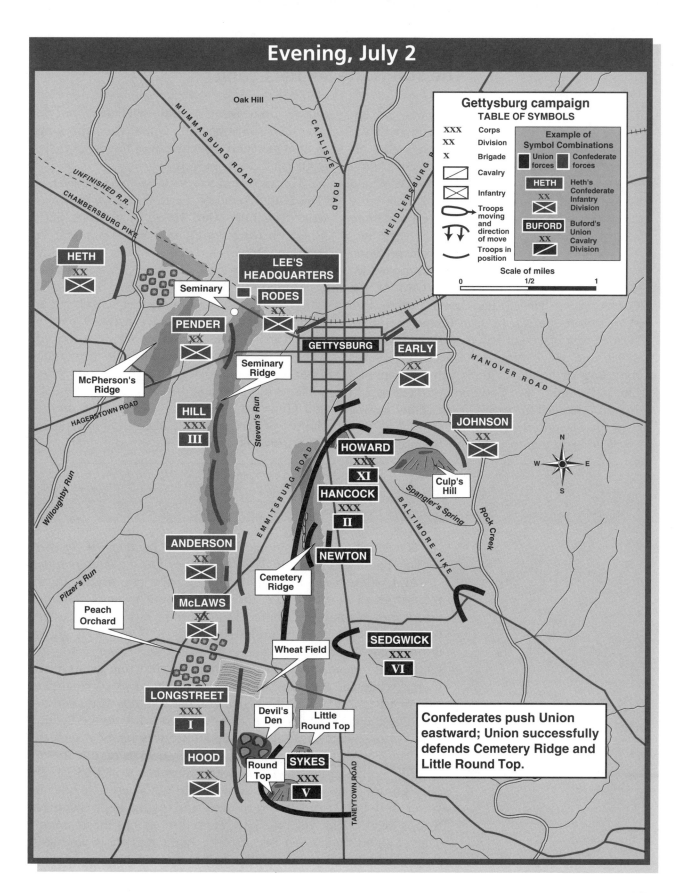

Confederates push Union eastward; Union successfully defends Cemetery Ridge and Little Round Top.

The Songs the Soldiers Sang

Music, particularly singing, was an important part of army life in both the North and the South. Songs such as "John Brown's Body," "Maryland, My Maryland," and "When Johnny Comes Marching Home" were popular around Civil War army camp fires and are still being played and sung today.

Many of the songs of the period were sung by both Federal and Confederate troops. Indeed, the unofficial national anthem of the Confederacy, "Dixie," had been written two years before the war by Dan Emmett of Ohio. "Dixie" was played at Jefferson Davis's inauguration and when Abraham Lincoln celebrated the news of Robert E. Lee's surrender. Sometimes, Northern and Southern soldiers would call an unofficial truce and join together to sing their favorite songs.

Soldiers sang to entertain themselves, to relieve homesickness and loneliness, and to raise their spirits before a battle. They also sang as they marched, the rhythm of the songs helping them to keep in step.

The most famous song of the Civil War is "The Battle Hymn of the Republic," which was written by Julia Ward Howe. It was first published in *The Atlantic Monthly* as a poem in February 1862, and Federal troops quickly picked up the words.

During the Battle of Gettysburg, jailers told Union prisoners in Libby Prison in Richmond, Virginia, that the Confederacy had just won a great victory. The prisoners were overjoyed when a black slave, who brought them their food, told them that the jailers were lying. Some of the prisoners began singing "The Battle Hymn of the Republic," all joining in on the chorus, "Glory, glory, hallelujah," and filling the prison with song.

Longstreet's worst fears had come true. The Army of Northern Virginia had taken heavy losses even as they lost the day's fighting.

And where were the commanders of the two armies during the battles of day two? Lee and Meade spent most of the afternoon and evening, as Confederate John B. Gordon wrote, "on opposite hills, . . . surrounded by staff . . . and with glasses [binoculars] in hand, . . . surveying the intervening space [the battlefield]." Meade took an active hand in directing troop movements, while Lee left those movements to his corps commanders.

As with most battles, the actual combat was not won or lost so much by the commanders but by the soldiers who did the fighting. One Texas soldier later said, "Every fellow was his own general." The Union soldiers proved to be the better generals on July 2.

The exhausted soldiers of both sides lay stretched on the hard ground. Those new to combat could not sleep. The cries for water and help from the wounded and dying kept the green troops awake. The veterans had learned to ignore these sounds. They wanted their sleep because the night was short, and soon they would face day three of the Battle of Gettysburg.

CHAPTER FIVE

Day Three: This Army Has Not Done Such Fighting as It Will Do Now

The third and final day of the Battle of Gettysburg, Friday, July 3, 1863, was the hottest and most humid of the conflict. The temperature climbed rapidly; by early afternoon it was close to ninety degrees, and the humidity was even higher. Combat under these conditions was like fighting in a steam room fully clothed.

This hothouse day was the climax of the Pennsylvania battle between the Army of the Potomac and the Army of Northern Virginia. General Robert E. Lee, who had made a number of serious errors during the previous two days of fighting, would make his worst mistake this day: He ordered an attack against the middle of Union-held Cemetery Ridge.

This assault, known as Pickett's charge, was the bloody climax of the whole battle. It was also one of the greatest military failures of all times. Lee and the Army of Northern Virginia lost the Battle of Gettysburg.

Meade and His Staff

Union commander George Meade began making his plans for July 3 the night before, just after the fighting for Cemetery and Culp's Hills finished. Meade, his corps leaders, and his staff officers met in the cramped front room of Meade's headquarters around 11:00 P.M. One Union officer later described these generals:

> [They were] as calm, as mild-mannered, and as free from flurry [turmoil] or excitement as a board of commissioners met to discuss a street improvement. . . . Some sat, some kept walking or standing, two lounged upon the bed, some were constantly smoking cigars.

Black Americans Fight for the Union

Although no African Americans fought at Gettysburg, many blacks enlisted and fought courageously for the Union. Slavery did not exist in the North, except in the border states of Delaware, Maryland, Kentucky, and Missouri, but racial prejudice did. At first the Federal army allowed blacks to serve only as laborers, not as combat soldiers. Black soldiers were paid less than white troopers, and they could not serve as officers.

Abolitionists won some reforms by the third year of the war. Black and white soldiers received equal pay, and black combat units were formed, under the command of white officers.

The most famous black regiment was the Fifty-fourth Massachusetts Infantry, which was headed by Colonel Robert Gould Shaw. Shaw was a member of one of the most active anti-slavery families in New England. Serving in the Fifty-fourth Massachusetts were two sons of Frederick Douglass, the former slave who had become one of America's most effective speakers and writers against slavery.

Shaw had difficulty winning the right for his men to fight. Finally, on July 18, 1863, the Fifty-fourth Massachusetts joined the attack on Fort Wagner, near Charleston, South Carolina. The Fifty-fourth, at the head of the attacking Federals, took heavy casualties and proved that African-American soldiers were as brave and capable as any of their white peers.

Among those killed was Colonel Shaw, who was buried in a mass grave with his men. This burial was meant as an insult by the Confederates, who were angry about the Union's using blacks in combat. Shaw's parents believed that their son would have wanted to be buried with the men that he had led and died with.

The Fifty-fourth Massachusetts's example spurred the creation of other black regiments. Before the war ended, over one hundred black units of infantry, cavalry, and artillery saw action.

An exhausted Gouverneur Warren, the Savior of Little Round Top, slept in a corner.

Meade had two important questions for his generals. First, should the Army of the Potomac remain where it was? All said yes. Second, should the Federals attack the Confederates or should they defend the ground that they now held? All voted to defend the Union army's present position. Meade was pleased with these answers because he had already written Washington that he intended to stay where he was and fight.

The generals also discussed possible avenues of retreat and the amount of food on hand before the meeting broke up around midnight. As the officers were leaving, Meade said to General John Gibbon of Second Corps, "If Lee attacks tomorrow, it will be in your front." Gibbon, who was acting as Second

Corps commander because Hancock was overseeing all the troops stationed on Cemetery Ridge and Little Round Top, asked how Meade could be so sure. "Because he [Lee] has made attacks on both our flanks and failed," answered the Northern commander, "and if he . . . [tries] again it will be on our center [where Second Corps is stationed]."

Lee's Plan

Meade was wrong, at least at that moment. Lee had spent the same evening thinking through his plans, and by midnight, he had decided to stick with his strategy of July 2. Ewell's Second Corps would continue the assault on Culp's Hill while Longstreet's First Corps would attack the Federal southern flank at the end of Cemetery Ridge once again.

Lee added one new wrinkle to the plan: a cavalry attack east of the Army of the Potomac aimed at cutting Meade's lines of communication with Washington, D.C. Lee once more had cavalry because late on the afternoon of the battle's second day General Jeb Stuart and the Army of Northern Virginia's cavalry finally returned.

When Stuart reported to Lee, the Southern commander, his face red in a rare display of anger, raised his arm as if to hit his cavalry chief. The cavalry general was surprised by Lee's anger, and hoping to overcome that anger, Stuart pointed to the wagons filled with supplies that his horse soldiers had captured, saying "I have brought you 125 wagons and their teams."

"Yes," said Lee, "but they are only an impediment [burden] to me now."

Lee's anger quickly passed. "Let me ask your [Stuart's] help now. We will not discuss this [Stuart's absence] longer. Help me fight these people [the Federals]."

Dawn Attack on Culp's Hill

Ewell, following Lee's written orders, sent four additional brigades to Johnson, whose division occupied a slice of Culp's Hill. Johnson was to use these reinforcements to make a dawn attack against the Union defenders, Slocum's Twelfth Corps. The division commander placed six brigades on the hill and kept two more below as reserves. However, the Federals struck before Johnson could make any other move.

General Alpheus Williams, Twelfth Corps's second in command, opened fire upon the Confederates with twenty-six artillery pieces that he had had dragged into position during the night. The artillery blasted away for fifteen minutes.

When the firing stopped, Johnson finally launched his attack. However, instead of ordering a mass attack, the Confederate general sent forward only one of his six brigades on Culp's Hill. Although this unit, the Stonewall Brigade, was made up of hardened, experienced veterans, a hail of Union bullets sent it reeling back. Only after the hurried retreat of the Stonewall Brigade did Johnson order his other units forward.

The Federals Win atop Culp's Hill

For the next several hours, the two sides engaged in a fierce shooting match. The Confederates used every possible tree and boulder for cover, but could not make any headway against the Federals. The bluecoated soldiers were well protected in their trenches or behind the log barricades that they had built two days before.

By midmorning Johnson sought to end this standoff and ordered his two reserve brigades to storm Culp's Hill. Both brigade commanders, Generals George H. Steuart and Junius Daniel, protested that the assault would be suicide, but Johnson ordered them to attack anyway.

As soon as the Federals saw the two brigades, the Union defenders on the hill opened up with rifle and cannon and cut Steuart's unit to pieces. Steuart's survivors retreated, and lacking their support, so did Daniel's men.

On the summit of Culp's Hill, Williams now ordered his own assault. His men scrambled out of their trenches and from behind their barricades, and within the hour they had driven the last Confederate off the hill. By noon the Second Corps's attack on Culp's Hill was over.

Longstreet Draws Up a Plan

The beginning of Johnson's fight for Culp's Hill was supposedly First Corps's signal to hit the Federals. However, Longstreet and his soldiers never attacked because orders never reached them. Lee appears not to have issued these orders, perhaps having changed his mind about the timing of the two assaults.

Longstreet had spent the night preparing a plan that would take his troops south around Round Top and then northwest to hit the Federals in their rear. Old Pete thought that the back of the Union line would prove much weaker than its front.

The First Corps commander was putting the finishing touches on this plan when Lee rode up, but Lee had no interest in Longstreet's scheme. The Southern commander still wanted Longstreet to launch an attack against the Federals' southern flank along the same route that Old Pete's men had followed the day before. Pointing to the northeast and echoing his previous words, Lee said, "The enemy is there, and I am going to strike him."

To Split the Federals' Center

Old Pete objected. He had failed to break the Federal flank when his soldiers were fresh, so how could he do so now? The men of Hood's and McLaws's divisions were still exhausted from yesterday's savage fighting.

After further discussion and thought, Lee finally agreed with Longstreet. Yes, the Federals' southern flank was too strong, but maybe the center of the Union line on Cemetery Ridge was not.

Lee believed that Meade had reinforced the troops on Culp's Hill and at the south end of the ridge with soldiers from units defending the Federal line's center. The Northern commander had strengthened his northern and southern flanks by robbing, and thus weakening, his center.

A hard blow to the weakened Federal center should split the Army of the Potomac in half. Lee was sure that his troops could then defeat the broken-backed Northern force.

Lee's plan was simple. The Confederate attackers would march from Seminary Ridge across bare, level farmland (about three-fifths of a mile) and then charge up the slope of Cemetery Ridge. Their only obstacle, although a major one, would be the constant fire from Federal infantry and artillery.

George H. Steuart's brigade renews its attack on Culp's Hill. Few would survive the reckless charge straight into Union fire.

Pickett's Charge, July 3

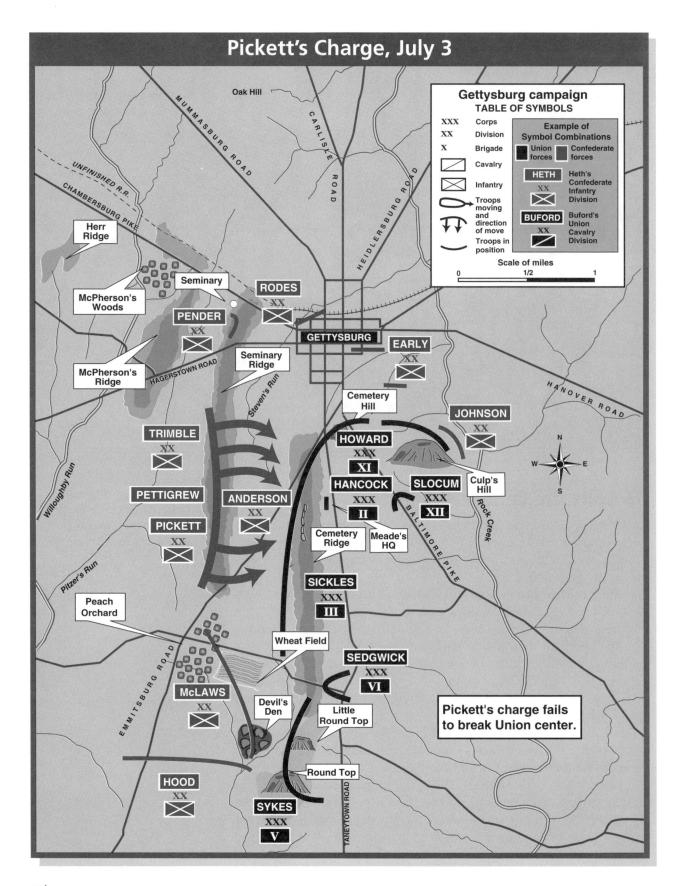

Gettysburg campaign
TABLE OF SYMBOLS

XXX	Corps
XX	Division
X	Brigade

Cavalry

Infantry

Troops moving and direction of move

Troops in position

Example of Symbol Combinations

Union forces | Confederate forces

HETH — Heth's Confederate Infantry Division

BUFORD — Buford's Union Cavalry Division

Scale of miles
0   1/2   1

Oak Hill

MUMMASBURG ROAD

CARLISLE ROAD

HEIDLERSBURG ROAD

UNFINISHED R.R.

CHAMBERSBURG PIKE

Herr Ridge

McPherson's Woods

Seminary

RODES
XX

PENDER
XX

Seminary Ridge

Steven's Run

McPherson's Ridge

HAGERSTOWN ROAD

GETTYSBURG

EARLY
XX

HANOVER ROAD

Cemetery Hill

JOHNSON
XX

TRIMBLE
XX

HOWARD
XXX
XI

HANCOCK
XXX
II

SLOCUM
XXX
XII

Culp's Hill

Rock Creek

Willoughby Run

PETTIGREW

ANDERSON
XX

PICKETT
XX

Cemetery Ridge

Meade's HQ

BALTIMORE PIKE

Pitzer's Run

SICKLES
XXX
III

Peach Orchard

Wheat Field

SEDGWICK
XXX
VI

EMMITSBURG ROAD

McLAWS
XX

Devil's Den

Little Round Top

Pickett's charge fails to break Union center.

HOOD
XX

Round Top

TANEYTOWN ROAD

SYKES
XXX
V

Pickett Directs the Charge

Eleven brigades, or thirteen thousand soldiers, were to make the charge. The core of the Confederate attack was to be the division led by General George E. Pickett of Longstreet's First Corps. Pickett's men were rested, having arrived too late on July 2 to do any fighting. Pickett, whose name would become forever linked with the charge that Lee now ordered, had been afraid that he would reach Gettysburg too late to take part in the battle.

The rest of the attacking troops came from Hill's Third Corps. They were the divisions of Generals W. Dorsey Pender and Henry Heth, which had seen little action the previous day. Both Pender and Heth were out of action, having been wounded, so Pickett would direct all three units. Longstreet would be in overall command of the attack.

The remainder of Longstreet's First Corps, Hood's and McLaws's divisions, were to act as support. Lee may have meant for these units to attack the Federals' southern line at the same

General Pickett accepts the order to charge from General Longstreet. Knowing the charge would be futile, Longstreet said, "There never was a body of thirteen thousand men who could make that attack successfully."

time as Pickett's troops charged. If so, the Confederate commander failed to make himself clear because Longstreet kept the two divisions back, waiting to see if Pickett's attack succeeded.

Longstreet Objects

Longstreet tried to argue Lee out of ordering this charge, which the First Corps commander said was doomed to failure. Old Pete told him:

> General, I have been a soldier all my life. . . . I have been with soldiers engaged in fights by . . . companies, regiments, divisions, and armies, and should know as well as anyone what soldiers can do. It is my opinion that no . . . [thirteen thousand] men ever arrayed [dressed] for battle can take that position.

> Lee's mind was made up, and nothing Longstreet could say would change it. The Southern commander was confident that soldiers of the Army of Northern Virginia could overrun the Federal center. As Heth later said, "The fact is, General Lee believed the Army of Northern Virginia, as it then existed, could accomplish anything." Despite the courage and steadfastness shown by the Army of the Potomac the previous day, Lee still believed that the Union soldiers were inferior to his own.

> Longstreet remained convinced that the undertaking would fail. "My heart was heavy," he later wrote. "I could see the desperate and hopeless nature of the charge and the hopeless slaughter it would cause. . . . That day at Gettysburg was one of the saddest of my life."

The Confederate Artillery Opens Fire

Lee may have been confident of his troops' fighting abilities, but he did not intend to send them against the Federal forces on Cemetery Ridge without help. That help was a massive artillery bombardment of Cemetery Ridge.

At a little after 1:00 P.M., some 140 Confederate cannons began roaring away at the Union troops on Cemetery Ridge. The guns formed a four-mile line that began north of Seminary Ridge and ended south of the ridge at the Peach Orchard that was the site of combat the previous day.

Making up the center of the Federal line was John Gibbon and two divisions of Second Corps. Thus, Meade's prediction of the night before was coming true. Gibbon's Second Corps was the target for one hundred Southern guns.

From Cemetery Ridge the entire line of Confederate artillery seemed to dissolve into flame and smoke. Army of the Potomac

Staying Calm

The two-hour Confederate artillery bombardment of Cemetery Ridge on the third day of the Battle of Gettysburg was frightening. The terrified Union soldiers wondered if anything could live through the storm of flying metal. Lee had hoped that the barrage would force the Federals from Second Corps to break and run.

To prevent a panic, many senior Union officers moved about and acted as normally as possible. By ignoring the flying and exploding shells, they hoped to steady their troops.

General John Gibbon and his aide Lieutenant Frank Haskell walked quietly along the lines and stopped to talk with crouching soldiers. General William Harrow paced coolly back and forth in front of his men. General Alexander Webb leaned casually on his sword and smoked a cigar.

Meanwhile, General Abner Doubleday of First Corps sat out on the ridge and ate his lunch. At one point a shell threw gravel on his sandwich, and the general laughed, saying, "That sandwich will need no salt." General Winfield Scott Hancock had been dictating an order for beef for Second Corps when the bombardment began. He calmly finished his dictation. Then Hancock mounted a black horse, checked to see that his uniform was neat, and rode out along Cemetery Ridge. Behind him came his staff. One officer that they passed protested, "General, the corps commander ought not to risk his life that way." Hancock answered, "There are times when a corps commander's life does not count."

Later, one Union soldier admitted that the sight of Hancock let him "find the courage to endure the pelting of the pitiless gale" of Confederate shells.

artillery chief, General Henry Hunt, watched from the top of Little Round Top and said that the sight was "indescribably grand."

Grand it might have been to Hunt, but not to those being hit. To the soldiers on Cemetery Ridge, it was a nightmare of pounding shells and cannon balls. Chaplain Alanson A. Haines of Sixth Corps later wrote:

> A terrible rain of hundreds of tons of iron missiles were hurled through the air. The forests crashed and the rocks were rent [broken] under the terrible hail . . . the smoke was impenetrable and rolled over the scene of action concealing all.

On Cemetery Ridge the bluecoated soldiers found shelter wherever they could. They burrowed into shallow trenches, crouched behind stone walls, and slid under fallen trees.

Hundreds died, and hundreds more were wounded. Men were pierced by fragments from exploding shells and speared by huge wooden splinters from trees that were blown apart. Artillery units died as Confederate shells set off gunpowder for Union cannons.

Hunt had given strict orders that only a few Federal artillery pieces were to return the Confederate fire. Meade's artillery chief was running low on ammunition, and he wanted to keep as much of it as he could for what was most likely coming, a mass infantry attack by the Army of Northern Virginia.

Pickett's Charge Begins

Despite the power of the Confederate bombardment, Federal casualties were light. The stone walls and shallow trenches on Cemetery Ridge proved good protection. Also, some of the Army of Northern Virginia's guns had been too far from their targets.

More importantly, many Confederate guns had fired too high, and their shells had fallen on the far side of Cemetery Ridge. This overshooting happened because thick smoke produced by the first few salvos hid the Union line from the Southern gunners. The latter then had to guess the location of their targets. Their guessing was none too accurate, and in the end, the Confederate shelling did little to weaken the Union defense.

After almost two hours, the cannons fell silent, and Longstreet reluctantly ordered Pickett to advance. The Confederate attackers, who had sat out the artillery bombardment behind Seminary Ridge, prepared themselves. They knew that this charge was going to be very dangerous. As one Tennessee sergeant said to his soldiers, "Boys, . . . it will be hot for us, and we will have to do our best." Officers gathered their troops together, some for prayer, some for patriotic speeches, and some for useful advice. Pickett's men finally started forward at 3:00 P.M.

The Federals Prepare to Fight

Federal lookouts on Little Round Top immediately spotted the mass of gray uniforms emerging from behind Seminary Ridge. The word spread quickly among the Union soldiers. "Here they come! Here they come! Here comes the infantry!"

Many bluecoated soldiers, as Lieutenant Colonel Edmund Rice wrote, were impressed by the sight of "the grandeur of [an] attack by so many thousand men." Lieutenant Frank Haskell was even more poetic when he later said that "the arms [weapons] of . . . [several] thousand men, barrel and bayonet, gleam in the sun, a sloping forest of flashing steel. Right on they move as with one soul."

As the Confederates marched at a steady pace of 110 steps a minute toward the Union line, the Federals got ready. Officers of Second Corps jammed as many men into the front line as possible. The rest waited close behind to provide replacements for fallen comrades or reinforcements where needed.

Artillery was moved forward. Major Alonzo Cushing, in charge of three guns, directed the placement of the cannons with one hand, while he used the other to keep his intestines from spilling out through a nasty belly wound.

Some fifty-seven hundred Union soldiers, five hundred gunners, and twenty-three cannons made a line three-fifths of a mile long.

Slaughter on the Battlefield

Pickett's men continued their steady march even when they began coming under early artillery fire. For twenty minutes, they kept their orderly ranks. Then, when they were less than a thousand feet from the Union line, they met a storm of cannon fire and broke rank.

Many of the Union cannons fired canister shot, which were cans filled with musket balls. Field guns shooting canisters were like giant shotguns that literally mowed down whole columns of men.

Regular exploding shells were just as deadly. One Confederate officer noted that "sometimes as many as ten men . . . [were] killed [or] wounded by the bursting of a single shell." General Richard Garnett and his horse were caught in one such blast. Only the bloodied horse emerged. Garnett's body was never found.

Pickett's men begin their charge. For a mile Pickett and his men kept on, facing the brutal fire of Hancock's infantry. Every one of Pickett's brigade commanders went down and their men fell by the hundreds around them.

Field Hospitals

Civil War soldiers on both sides were afraid of their military doctors. One Alabama soldier said, "I believes [sic] the doctors kill more than they cure," and an Illinois private observed, "Our doctor knows about as much as a ten year old boy."

And these soldiers had good reason for their fears. Medical knowledge was still primitive. Doctors had chloroform and ether to knock out their patients during surgery and opium to control pain. However, they had no antibiotics to stop the infections that killed a lot of soldiers.

Soldiers shot in the body generally died. Those shot in arms or legs had a better chance of living—if they survived the amputation. The wounded man was placed on a table covered with a rubber sheet. Even if no anesthesia was available, the shattered limb was cut off. The wounded man, often screaming and thrashing about, was held down by surgical assistants.

No one knew about germs at this period, so nothing was kept clean. Between operations the rubber sheet might or might not be sponged off. The surgeon would rinse his scalpel in a pan of bloody water and then wipe it dry with a dirty rag.

Even getting from the battlefield to the hospital was not easy. It was not until the middle of the war that either side created a corps of medics whose only job was to cart the wounded to field hospitals. Before then, the wounded might be picked up by members of the regimental band, or they might not be picked up at all. At times, the wounded might lie for hours, sometimes even a day, before help arrived.

A surgeon prepares to amputate the limb of a fallen soldier in this rare photograph of a Civil War field hospital. With very few ways of fighting infection, the most common method of "curing" a soldier who had suffered a leg wound was to amputate.

As groups of Confederates reached the bottom of Cemetery Ridge, the Federals met them with volley after volley of rifle fire. In the slaughter that followed, only a small number of Southern soldiers even reached the top of the ridge.

Of the entire Twenty-sixth North Carolina Regiment, for example, only 2 soldiers made it to the Union line. Badly outnumbered, they surrendered immediately. In another instance, the 150 men of the Forty-seventh North Carolina Regiment were pinned to the slope of Cemetery Ridge. Unable to advance or retreat, they also surrendered.

Confederate and Union troops engage in fighting on the last day of the Battle of Gettysburg.

The Struggle at the Angle

Only once did any of Pickett's men come close to breaking through the Federal line. This was at the Angle. The Union defenders at the northern end of the Second Corps line crouched behind a stone wall, which ran south and then jogged west to avoid a clump of trees. The Angle was the spot where the wall turned.

General Lewis Armistead led some 350 Confederates in a rush against the Angle and its Union defenders. The Seventy-first Pennsylvania Regiment bolted as the Southern soldiers, bellowing out the rebel yell, swarmed over the stone wall.

The remaining Federals fought desperately to hold the Confederates at bay. In the ensuing fight, attackers killed Alonzo Cushing and overran his artillery equipment.

The place where Pickett made his valiant charge. After the suicidal effort, Lee, with hat in hand, would tell Pickett, "It was all my fault. Now help me save that which remains."

Just as it seemed that the Confederates would pierce the Union line, Federal reinforcements directed by Hancock and Gibbon raked the attackers with rifle and artillery fire. In the fierce fighting that followed, Armistead was mortally wounded and his soldiers were killed, driven off, or captured. On the Federal side, both Hancock and Gibbon were wounded seriously enough to be carried from the battlefield.

Pickett's Charge Ends

At the time, the possibility of Armistead and his troops, bursting through the Union line appeared to threaten the whole Federal army. In fact, it did not. First, the Confederates numbered only a few hundred, and they would have gotten no help from other Southern soldiers, most of whom had either been killed or driven back. Second, when Meade heard of the threatened breakthrough, he ordered his thirteen thousand reserve soldiers forward. The force was more than enough to subdue Armistead and his men.

As the Federals cleared out the Angle, Pickett's men were beginning their retreat. Union artillery continued to hammer at the Southern soldiers until they reached the safety of Seminary Ridge.

It was now 4:00 P.M., and Pickett's charge had ended in complete disaster. In an hour of fighting, Pickett had lost over half his command. Some sixty-five hundred attackers had been killed or wounded, while many others had been captured. In contrast, the Federals had sustained only fifteen hundred casualties.

Pickett's charge was the last major fighting of the day and of the Pennsylvania conflict. The Battle of Gettysburg was over, and the Army of the Potomac had won.

In Victory . . .

The soldiers and officers of the Army of the Potomac were elated with their victory over their old enemy, the Army of Northern Virginia. Lieutenant Jesse Young of Third Corps reported that "cheer after cheer rose from the triumphant boys in blue, echoing from Round Top, reechoing from Cemetery Ridge, . . . making the very heavens throb." Even normally quiet George Meade stood cheering and waving with his troops as Pickett's men retreated.

The soldiers were the most enthusiastic about Hancock and the Second Corps commander's role in the battle. They mobbed his hospital bed. Hancock tried to make a speech but passed out from his painful wound.

No single officer or soldier won the Battle of Gettysburg. It was the entire Army of the Potomac. As historian Albert Nofi observes:

> It was the *Army of the Potomac* itself that was the victor. A fine, skilled, professional force, Gettysburg was the first battle in which it was ably led on all levels and permitted to fight to the end. . . . When Meade gave them their chance, they took it. Almost everyone had performed well, occasionally magnificently.

. . . and Defeat

Across the flat Pennsylvania farmland on Seminary Ridge, emotions were different. This third and final day of the conflict had not been a good one for Lee, Pickett, or the soldiers of the Army of Northern Virginia. Union troops stopped even Jeb Stuart.

After the disaster of Pickett's charge, Lee was heard to cry out, "Too bad! *Too bad!* Oh, too bad!" He met the survivors of the ill-fated charge as they staggered back to Confederate lines and apologized to them. "It's all my fault," Lee said. "It is I who have lost this fight."

Lee had misjudged both his army and that of Meade's. As Colonel William C. Oates of the Fifteenth Alabama Regiment would later observe, "He [Lee] was overconfident." Pickett, who

Clara Barton

Clara Barton, known as "The Angel of the Battlefield," was one of the most famous nurses of the Civil War. Born in 1821 in Oxford, Massachusetts, the former teacher was working as a clerk in the Patent Office when the war began.

Barton first treated wounded soldiers in 1861 when Federal troops, who had been attacked by Southern sympathizers in Baltimore, were brought to Washington, D.C.

Barton personally took medicines and supplies to frontline soldiers, thus earning her nickname. In September 1862 she followed the Army of the Potomac's Second Corps into battle at Antietam, driving a wagon onto the battlefield. There she helped doctors treat the wounded, at one point even removing a bullet from the cheek of a soldier. One of the Union doctors she was helping was shot dead while they worked.

Near the end of the war, Lincoln asked Barton to compile a list of missing and dead soldiers. This job took her to the notorious Confederate prison of Andersonville, where she recorded the names of hundreds of Union prisoners of war who had died there.

After the Civil War, Clara Barton joined the International Red Cross and aided the

Clara Barton worked so close to the front lines that at Antietam a stray bullet passed through her sleeve and killed the soldier she was caring for.

wounded in the 1870 Franco-Prussian War. In 1881 she founded the American Red Cross and served as its president until 1904. She expanded the organization's role to include help for those caught in natural disasters as well as war. She died in 1912.

---

had lost two-thirds of his division would also blame Lee, saying "That old man . . . had my division massacred."

However, such thoughts would come later. Now, all Pickett could remember were the ghosts of the fallen. As he wrote to his fiancée that night:

> I can still hear them [his soldiers] cheering as I gave the order, "Forward!" The thrill of their joyous voices as they called out, "We'll follow you, Marse [Master] George, we'll follow you!" On, how faithfully they followed me on, on to their death, and I led them on, on, on, Oh God!"

CONCLUSION

The End of Battle and Afterwards: We All Remember Gettysburg

The Battle of Gettysburg was over. The Civil War was not. The Army of Northern Virginia may have lost the battle, but it still remained an intact and dangerous fighting force. The Army of the Potomac may have won the battle, but it had sustained serious damage in the conflict.

Yet, this three-day Pennsylvania battle was an important turning point in the war. Confederate leaders had hoped to gain much from Lee's invasion of the Northern states: relief for the besieged Mississippi city of Vicksburg, help from England and France, and perhaps even an end to the war on Southern terms. None of these things came to pass, and because they did not, the Union, not the Confederacy, eventually won the Civil War.

Meade Refuses to Counterattack

In the late afternoon of July 3, 1863, no one, including Lee and Meade, knew that the fighting at Gettysburg was over. As soon as Pickett's men began drifting back to the Confederate lines, Lee prepared for an attack by the cheering Federals. That assault never came.

Several Union officers, among them Hancock, urged Meade to send Federal troops across the crushed farm fields to Seminary Ridge to attack the Confederates, but the Northern commander decided against such a counterattack. First, Meade knew that the Army of Northern Virginia was still dangerous.Most of Longstreet's First Corps and Ewell's Second Corps had done no fighting that day and were still fresh enough to resist.

After Gettysburg, Major General George Meade decided against attacking Lee to finish off the Army of Northern Virginia. Lincoln always regretted that he had not personally gone to Gettysburg to urge Meade on. The war would last another two years.

In contrast, all of the Army of the Potomac soldiers were exhausted from three days of heavy fighting. Even the reserve troops were tired from having made forced marches to reach Gettysburg in time.

Second, Meade could see that the Confederate artillery was still in place. Although Meade suspected that Lee's field guns were low on shells, the Northern general also believed that they still had plenty of canister shot, the same ammunition that had caused such destruction to Pickett and his men.

Meade was right in his guesses about the Southern artillery. The Confederate gunners would have liked nothing better than a chance to fire at attacking Federals.

Waiting Out Lee

Meade decided to be cautious. He and the Army of the Potomac would remain where they were.

Meade had no way of knowing if Lee would launch another all-out attack against the Northern force, but if the Confederates came again, the Army of the Potomac was in the best place to meet an assault. Three days of Confederate failure to take the Union-held heights showed the wisdom of remaining in place.

Meade was expecting both fresh supplies and reinforcements to arrive within days. At that time, if Lee and his army were still across the valley, the Army of the Potomac could attack. Until then, as he told his officers, "We have done well enough."

Lee Retreats

Lee did not attack again nor did he wait for Meade to be reinforced. On the evening of July 4, Independence Day, the Army of Northern Virginia began slipping out of its Gettysburg camp and heading south for Virginia. Heavy rain hid the army's retreat.

Lee was forced to leave seven thousand of his most badly wounded men to become Union prisoners. To have taken them along would have slowed the Confederates down and put the whole army at risk.

Meade quickly learned of the Southern withdrawal and eventually pursued Lee. The Northern commander, still very cautious, was slow in his pursuit of the Army of Northern Virginia. He caught up with the Southern force on the banks of the Potomac, not far from the old Antietam battlefield in Maryland.

Meade proposed to his corps commanders that the Army of the Potomac attack the Army of Northern Virginia on July 13. All but two of the corps leaders voted the idea down, believing such an attack was too dangerous.

Meade had been leading the Northern army for only two weeks and still did not have a feel for his new command. Therefore, he had no choice but to go along with this vote. As Meade wrote the Federal army command in Washington, D.C., "I do not wish to imitate his [Lee's] example at Gettysburg and assault a position where the chances were so greatly against success."

And, indeed, such an attack might have been foolish. Lee expected an assault and had his soldiers dig trenches and build barricades. Lee's preparations would have made any attack a costly one.

When the Southern commander saw that the Army of the Potomac was not going to attack, he and his men crossed over the Potomac and marched toward the Shenandoah Valley. Meade followed.

Lee's stubborness at Gettysburg would result in the loss of more than a third of his army and any hope that the Confederates would win the war.

The Gettysburg Campaign Ends

Lincoln was furious with Meade when he learned that Lee had escaped back into Virginia. The president wrote:

> My dear general, I . . . believe you appreciate the magnitude of the misfortune involved in Lee's escape. He was within your easy grasp, and to have closed upon him would . . . have ended the war.

Lincoln later came to see that he had unfairly criticized Meade. The Army of the Potomac commander could not afford to lose a major battle to Lee on Union soil. Indeed, Meade had been ordered by his superiors in Washington to "maneuver and fight in such a manner as to cover the capital and Baltimore." A defeat to Lee would have put both cities at risk.

There were no more chances to corner and fight the Army of Northern Virginia once it reached the Shenandoah Valley. Except for some minor skirmishes, the two armies did no more fighting that summer. On July 24, the Army of Northern Virginia made camp at Culpeper, Virginia, just south of the Rappahannock River and near the cavalry battle site of Brandy Station. The Army of the Potomac stopped and camped on the other side of the river, five miles from the Southern army. After two months of marching and fighting, the two armies were back where they started. Gettysburg was over.

The Price of Gettysburg

The three days of fighting at Gettysburg cost both armies a horrible price in human lives. The Army of the Potomac lost twenty-three thousand soldiers, about one-quarter of its men, while the Army of Northern Virginia had twenty-eight thousand casualties, one-third of the Southern troops who had followed Lee north.

At the end of the third day's fighting, the battlefield was a nightmare. The wounded lay everywhere. Union lieutenant Jesse Young saw

> thousands of men . . . lying unattended, scattered over the field, mingled with broken gun carriages, . . . hundreds of dead and dying horses, and other ghastly debris of the battlefield. . . . Relays of men with stretchers . . . passed . . . with their bloody freight, now and then a groan or a suppressed shriek telling the story of suffering. . . . It was a sight . . . long to be remembered.

The dead also were everywhere. From the Confederate camp, artillery gunner Robert Stiles saw the dead bodies of men and horses [that] had lain there putrefying [rotting] under the summer sun for three days. The sights and smells that assailed us were simply indescribable—corpses swollen to twice their original size, some of them . . . burst asunder [apart] with the pressure of foul gases and vapors. . . . Several . . . corpses sat upright against a fence, with arms extended in the air and faces hideous with something very like a fixed leer.

The Northern army could and would replace its losses easily. The Southern army could not. As Lee wrote Confederate president Davis, "Though conscious that the enemy has been much shattered in the recent battle, I am aware that he can be easily reinforced, while no addition can be made to our numbers." The defeat was a disaster for the Confederacy for many reasons but particularly for the human loss.

(Right) Men of the Twenty-fourth Michigan Regiment lie dead on the field of battle. This regiment left seven distinct rows of dead as it fell back from battle line to battle line. Three-fourths of its numbers would perish. (Below) The wounded are carried off the battlefield. The South would not recover from the losses suffered at Gettysburg.

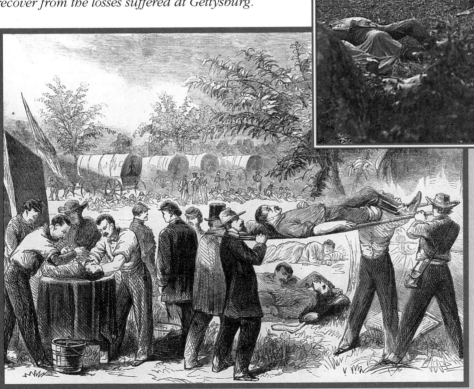

The New York Draft Riots

On Sunday, July 12, 1863, a week after the Battle of Gettysburg, the worst riot in the history of the United States broke out in New York City. The rioters were workers who were angry about being drafted to free the slaves in the South. The rioters believed that they would lose their jobs to these freed blacks because employers could pay them lower wages.

For four days, mobs of angry men and women roamed the streets. They burned federal buildings, particularly draft offices. They attacked the office of any newspaper, such as the New York Tribune, that supported the war.

African Americans were also targets of the rioters. The mobs lynched half a dozen blacks and beat up many more. They wrecked black homes and property and even burned one African-American orphanage to the ground.

The New York police force, unable to control the rioting, asked the army for help. However, most army units were in Pennsylvania chasing Lee and the Army of Northern Virginia.

Several regiments were ordered to New York. When they arrived on July 15, the veteran combat troops opened fire on the rioters. Their deadly rifle volleys had much the same effect on the mobs as they had had on charging Confederates at Gettysburg. Within a day, the riots were over. The final death toll was well over a hundred.

The Confederacy Loses Another Battle

Lee's defeat in Pennsylvania shocked the South. Public confidence that had been high before the invasion dropped sharply. "This [is] the darkest hour of the war," wrote Confederate War Department clerk John Jones. "The news from Lee's army is appalling."

Southern morale took another beating when bad news from the west reached the eastern states. On July 4, the day Lee began his retreat from Gettysburg, Vicksburg and an entire Confederate army surrendered to Ulysses S. Grant. The whole Mississippi River was now in the hands of the Union. Grant had done to the Confederacy what Lee had failed to do with the Army of the Potomac: He had split it in half.

The Confederacy, which seemed to have been doing so well in the war a month before, was now in obvious trouble. Confederate general Josiah Gorgas wrote:

Events have succeeded one another with disastrous rapidity. One month ago we were apparently at the point of success. . . . Now the picture is just as somber as it was bright then. . . . Yesterday we rode on the pinnacle [summit] of success—today absolute ruin seems to be our portion.

Taking the Blame

No one took the defeat at Gettysburg harder than Lee, who insisted on taking the blame for the defeat. "The army did all it could," he wrote. "I fear I required of it impossibilities." Later, he would add, "I have no complaints to make of anyone but myself."

On August 8, Lee sent Davis a letter offering to resign as commander of the Army of Northern Virginia. Lee said that a commander who is no longer trusted must be replaced:

I have heard and seen . . . discontent in the public journals [newspapers] at the result of the expedition [northern invasion]. I do not know how far this feeling extends in the army. . . . It is fair . . . to suppose that it does exist. . . . Everything points to the advantages . . . [of] a new commander.

Davis immediately sent Lee a letter urging the latter to remain in command. As Davis pointed out, "To ask me to [find a] substitute [for] you . . . is to demand of me an impossibility." The Confederate president's letter ended Lee's talk of resigning.

The Confederacy Stands Alone

Lee's defeat at Gettysburg ended any chance that either England or France would recognize the Confederacy as an independent nation. Nor would either country supply food, arms, or equipment.

Andersonville

Both Union and Confederate forces captured thousands of enemy soldiers during the four years of fighting. These prisoners were jammed into overcrowded prison camps.

The worst of these camps was the Confederacy's Andersonville prison in Georgia. Set up in early 1864, this military prison was never meant to hold more than ten thousand prisoners, yet by the summer of 1864, Andersonville's population topped thirty-two thousand. Some fifty thousand prisoners were confined there before the war's end; one-third of these men died.

Eliza Andrews, a Georgia woman, left the following account of Andersonville:

During the summer the wretched prisoners burrowed in the ground like moles to protect themselves from the sun. . . . These underground huts . . . were alive with vermin and stank like charnel houses. Many of the prisoners were stark naked. . . . At one time the prisoners died at the rate of a hundred and fifty a day. . . . Dysentery was the most fatal disease, and . . . they [the prisoners] lay . . . in their own excrement.

Andrews points out that the conditions at Andersonville and other Confederate prisons were the result of the massive shortages of food and medicine in the South. Still, the suffering of Union prisoners at Andersonville was so great that the camp's commanding officer, Captain Henry Wirz, was eventually tried and executed after the war.

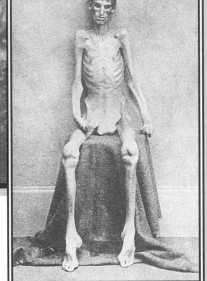

(Above) Soldiers bury their own in a long trench that would soon be filled with dead at Andersonville. (Right) A Union soldier, still alive, stares out in silent testimony to the unremitting cruelty of the prison camps.

Fifty Years Later

The wounds of the Civil War were a long time in healing, particularly in the South. The war left the former Confederacy in shambles; its society and customs were gone forever. In addition, the military occupation of the south lasted another decade.

Veteran groups formed in both the North and South, yet they remained small for several decades after the war. Most northern and southern veterans wanted to escape the horrors of the war, not remember them. The southerners were also haunted by their defeat. However, eventually the pain associated with the veterans' memories faded, and survivors flocked to join their old comrades.

As the pain of war passed, so did much of the bitterness. In 1913 Northern and Southern veteran groups joined together to show their restored unity. Fifty-four thousand Civil War veterans met in July of that year at Gettysburg to commemorate the fiftieth anniversary of the battle. This time the former soldiers came in peace, not war.

On July 3, 180 Federal veterans formed a line along Cemetery Ridge in the position that they had defended fifty years before. On the flat farmland in front of them a line of 120 Confederate survivors of Pickett's charge marched quietly forward. When they reached the Union veterans, the Southerners reached out and shook hands with their former foes. Onlookers cheered.

As Henry Adams, the son of the U.S. minister to England, wrote, "It is now conceded that all hope for [English and French] intervention [in the war] is at an end."

Without this outside help, shortages in the South became worse, particularly as the Union blockade tightened around the Confederate seacoast. The lengthening war drained the desperate South's few remaining resources. And with the Confederate defeats and Union victories at Gettysburg and Vicksburg, the war was going to continue. As historian Albert Nofi observes:

> The Confederate loss at Gettysburg meant that the war would go on. The South would never again have so fine an army as that which marched north . . . in June of 1863, while the armies of the Republic [the Union] would continue to grow stronger and better. In a protracted [drawn-out] war, the greater material resources of the Union would inevitably triumph.

Indeed, the future of the Confederacy looked so dark that Davis sent his vice president under a white flag of truce to see if he could bargain with Lincoln. The U.S. president refused to see the Southern messenger. Josiah Gorgas observed, "The Confederacy totters to its destruction."

The Union After Gettysburg

The victory at Gettysburg, particularly when combined with the fall of Vicksburg, showed that the Union could win the battles needed to win the war. Only a month before, Northerners had all but given up on the Federal army and the war. Now they were saying that the Union could and would win.

For the first time since early in 1861, morale in the North was good. In a telegram to Meade one Union officer said: "The glorious success of the Army of the Potomac has electrified all." In Northern cities, wrote Captain William Thompson Lusk, "Bells are ringing wildly. . . . Citizens grin at one another with fairly idiotic smiles. . . . All hysterical nonsense is pardonable now."

In Support of the War

The Gettysburg and Vicksburg victories also helped give Lincoln a tighter political grip on the North. "Government is strengthened four-fold at home and abroad," wrote one enthusiastic New York Republican. "Copperheads are palsied [paralyzed] and dumb for the moment at least."

Lincoln's new political clout was shown that fall when Republicans swept all the state elections. In Ohio, Peace Democrat Clement L. Vallandigham, one of the loudest critics of the war, lost the governorship by 100,000 votes. Only 6 percent of the Union soldiers who voted supported Vallandigham and his call for an immediate end to the war.

The message was clear. Voters in the North, both civilian and military, wanted the war to continue. They were willing to put up with the sacrifices needed to bring the secessionist South back into the Union.

Lincoln summed up this feeling when, on November 19, 1863, he spoke at the ceremony dedicating Gettysburg as a permanent cemetery for the soldiers who had died there. In his now famous Gettysburg Address, he said, "It is for us . . . to be dedicated . . . to the great task remaining before us . . . that this nation . . . shall have a new birth."

Lincoln dedicates Gettysburg as a permanent cemetery for the soldiers who died there.

For Further Reading

Jack Coggins, *Arms and Equipment of the Civil War*. New York: The Fairfax Press, 1962. Provides good, detailed information on Union and Confederate weapons, uniforms, and equipment and explains the organization and duties of the infantry, cavalry, signal corps, the engineers, and so on. The author's vivid and historically accurate illustrations highlight the text.

Stephen Crane, *The Red Badge of Courage*. New York: Bantam Classics, 1981. This classic novel presents a graphic and realistic picture of the Civil War battlefield. In clear, vivid words, the author relates a young recruit's first day in combat.

Philip Katcher, *The Civil War Source Book*. New York: Facts On File, 1992. Ten sections and several hundred entries furnish worthwhile information on many aspects of the Civil War, such as camp life, military prisons, military salaries, and battlefield medicine, and includes biographies of major historical figures, photographs, maps, a glossary, and a bibliography.

Joe Kirchberger, *The Civil War and Reconstruction*. New York: Facts On File, 1991. A good, short history of the Civil War and its aftermath that is enriched by many passages taken from letters, diaries, and newspapers of the time. Photographs, maps, and a bibliography also support the text.

Robert Hunt Rhodes, ed., *All for the Union*. New York: Crown, 1991. A firsthand account of the everyday life of a Union soldier as told through the letters and diary of Elisha Hunt Rhodes, who joined the army as a nineteen-year-old private. He fought in every major eastern battle from First Bull Run to Appomattox.

Annette Tapert, ed., *The Brothers' War: Civil War Letters to Their Loved Ones from the Blue and Gray*. New York: Random House, 1988. A collection of letters by both Union and Confederate soldiers that reveals how these men saw the war in which they fought.

Geoffrey C. Ward et al., *The Civil War: An Illustrated History*. New York: Knopf, 1991. Lavishly illustrated with photographs, drawings, and maps, this companion volume to the PBS Civil War series presents a solid, short history of the conflict.

Manfred Weidhorn, *Robert E. Lee*. New York: Macmillan, 1988. A good, balanced biography of Lee that looks at both his military achievements and failures. The book describes Lee's prewar military career and his role in post–Civil War America. It is filled with photographs and maps and includes a bibliography.

Works Consulted

Bruce Catton, *This Hallowed Ground: The Story of the Union Side of the Civil War*. New York: Doubleday, 1956. A good, readable, short history of the Civil War, written by one of the foremost authorities on the period.

Henry Steele Commager, ed., *The Blue and the Gray: Two Volumes in One: The Story of the Civil War as Told by Participants*. New York: The Fairfax Press, 1960. An excellent collection of original writings from the Civil War. This illustrated collection is divided into sections that cover the important campaigns and battles, camp life, and Civil War songs. There are several useful maps and a detailed bibliography.

Shelby Foote, *The Civil War: A Narrative: Fredericksburg to Meridian*. New York: Vintage Books, 1963. This is the second in a three-volume work that is a thorough, elegantly written military history of the Civil War. It covers the Gettysburg campaign in great detail and with considerable insight.

The Gettysburg Papers, 2 vols. Compiled by Ken Bandy and Florence Freeland. Dayton, OH: Press of Morningside Bookshop, 1978. An excellent source of nineteenth-century writings about Gettysburg. Many of the authors fought in the battle.

James M. McPherson, ed., *The Atlas of the Civil War*. New York: Macmillan, 1994. An excellent resource that is filled with good, large maps in color and well-reproduced black-and-white photographs from the Civil War. Informative essays accompany the maps and review the events during each year of the Civil War. There is also a selected bibliography.

——, *Battle Cry of Freedom: The Civil War Era*. Oxford: Oxford University Press, 1988. A very good one-volume history of the Civil War by a prominent historian of the period. Generous use of quotations and a good bibliography strengthen the text.

Albert A. Nofi, *The Gettysburg Campaign: June-July 1863*, rev. ed. Conshohocken, PA: Combined Books, 1993. A good, general account of the Gettysburg campaign by a noted military historian. Several detailed maps of the battle and a thorough bibliography complement the narrative.

Stewart Sifakis, *Who Was Who in the Civil War*. New York: Facts On File, 1988. Provides much interesting and worthwhile information on some twenty-five hundred individuals who served the Union or the Confederacy. A timeline, illustrations, and photographs enrich the text.

Gene Smith, *Lee and Grant: A Dual Biography*. New York: McGraw-Hill, 1984. A good, general biography of the most important Confederate and Federal generals. Their stories are told in alternating chapters, and a good bibliography supports the text.

Richard Wheeler, ed., *Voices of the Civil War*. New York: Thomas Y. Crowell, 1976. A good sampling of original writings from the Civil War. The selections are divided by campaign and battle and are accompanied by a timeline and a bibliography.

Index

Picture Credits

Cover photo by Peter Newark's Military Pictures

About the Author

James A. Corrick has been a professional writer and editor for more than fifteen years and is the author of a dozen books, as well as close to two hundred articles and short stories. His most recent books are *Mars, Muscular Dystrophy*, and two other titles for Lucent Books: *The Early Middle Ages* and *The Late Middle Ages*. Corrick holds a doctorate in English, and his diverse academic background includes a graduate degree in the biological sciences. He has taught English, tutored minority students, edited three magazines for the National Space Society, and written science articles for the Muscular Dystrophy Association. He lives in Tucson, Arizona, with a constantly changing number of dogs and books. When not writing, Corrick reads, swims, lifts weights, takes long walks, frequents bookstores, and holds forth on any number of topics. He is a member of the Arizona Historical Society and the past secretary of the Tucson Book Publishing Association.